MW01535141

SOME SOUND, INSPIRING ADVICE FROM SOL GORDON:

JOYS can be shared; suffering cannot.

FEEL SORRY for people who (1) can't say thank you (2) don't understand that sometimes telling the truth is an expression of hostility.

NO ONE can make you feel inferior without *your* consent.

5 THINGS TO DO WHEN YOU'RE BORED: (1) Make friends—lovers come and go (2) Learn something well (3) Listen to music carefully (4) Enjoy nature (5) Remember that people who are bored are BORING.

ANTICIPATIONS are invariably more exciting than what happens. If the real thing comes remotely close, *live with it.*

WORRYING is good for you. Sometimes.

GETTING IT TOGETHER IS LIFE ITSELF.

Bantam Books by Sol Gordon, Ph.D.

THE NEW YOU
YOU WOULD IF YOU LOVED ME

THE NEW YOU

by Sol Gordon, Ph.D.

BANTAM BOOKS · NEW YORK · LONDON

THE NEW YOU
A Bantam Book / June 1979

All rights reserved.
Copyright © 1979 by Sol Gordon
This book may not be reproduced in whole or in part, by
mimeograph or any other means, without permission.
For information address: Bantam Books, Inc.

ISBN 0-553-12969-4

Published simultaneously in the United States and Canada

Bantam Books are published by Bantam Books, Inc. Its trademark, consisting of the words "Bantam Books" and the por-
trayal of a bantam, is Registered in U.S. Patent and Trademark
Office and in other countries. Marca Registrada. Bantam
Books, Inc., 666 Fifth Avenue, New York, New York 10019.

PRINTED IN THE UNITED STATES OF AMERICA

The new me
    dedicates the new you
to
        Judith
        and
            our
                son
    Josh

TABLE OF LIFE

Everybody's life can be sorted out in
eighteen parts but only
    if one part can be designated
as
    Things and stuff or
    miscellaneous

    (Until I begin again)

THE NEW YOU

FORWARD

Wisdom is learning what to overlook.
—William James

HOW IS THIS
SELF-IMPROVEMENT BOOK
DIFFERENT FROM OTHER
SELF-IMPROVEMENT BOOKS?

Other self-improvement books tell you

Not to worry. (When's the last time someone
told you to stop worrying and you
stopped?)
Not to feel guilty. (If you've done something
wrong, why shouldn't you feel guilty?)
That you can be anything you want to be.
(You should live so long.)
To get rid of unrealistic expectations. (How
does one know in advance that one's
expectations are unrealistic?)
That if you eliminate shoulds, musts,
perfectionistic tendencies, worries, and
other imperfections you'll be happy. (So,
what else is new?)

The plain fact is that

Life, in large part, is made up of things to
worry about,
not only personal things
but the state of the world,
like hunger, overpopulation, torture,
crime-infested cities; disasters occur,
personal tragedies—despair;
life can also be unfair, unlucky, uninteresting,
unnerving

for large parts of the day
or for years.

Real people have bad moods,
periods of depression,
fall in love with someone who doesn't love
them.

Real people very seldom are or become their
dreams and fantasies of what they want to be.

Life has disappointments, unwelcome
intrusions, boring tasks, unlucky breaks,
accidents, prolonged bouts of bad weather,
and physical ailments, to say nothing of being
oneself seriously handicapped.

For many, long periods on welfare, unhappy
marriages, ungrateful children.

Of course, there are joys and pleasures and
excitements and orgasms. But these are
occasional except when they dominate
memories of good old days.

All other self-improvement books want you
to pretend that you are the only reality. This
book does not pretend. It acknowledges the
pain of the real world, but it also says that

Optimism is easier than pessimism.

Wisdom, daydreaming, and risk taking
introduce you to options that you never
felt possible.

If you are reasonably secure about yourself and have neat visions about the directions you want to go, then you are less likely to exploit anyone else along your path than a person who feels inferior or supervulnerable.

I hope, anyway.

So just hang,
      not up,
      not out,
   not around,
   but in there,

   and see what happens.

LIFE
SECTION

*I have learned one
important thing in my life
—how to begin again.*
—Sam Keen

EIGHTEEN SLOGANS, POEMS, AND THINGS

New journeys, experiences, and people call forth a *New You*. Why eighteen? In biblical Hebrew, the word *chai* means life and its numerical value is eighteen. Life is my favorite number.

1. The existential question is coming to terms with life—not death.

2. You cannot find yourself

>> in a mirror
> or by
>> dieting
>> meditating
>> getting laid
>> announcing your rebirth
>> jogging
>> marrying
>> making money
> or at
>> discos
>> bars
>> churches
>> movies
>> races
>> steam baths
> nor in
>> front of TV
> only by
> letting yourself

be tried
and tested
in relationships with people.

3. An untested find (a sure cure, religion, inner peace) soon becomes a fad, a farce, or a weapon used against people who don't share your views.

4. People who feel good about themselves (most of the time) are not available for exploitation and have no desire to exploit others.

5. Not everything in life can be understood or resolved. All of us have some areas of vulnerability. Sometimes the best we can do isn't good enough.

6. Really marvelous experiences occur infrequently, are of brief duration, and are rarely on schedule.

7. If God wants to test you, what will you do?

8. Who among us
has not been evil?
The best that can be said
of the best among us
is that they have done
the best they could.

9. If you have a tendency to be self-deprecating, don't tell anyone. It's really boring to be with people who think they're boring.

10. One of the most difficult problems for

some people to face is the fact that their parents
are nice people.

11. It's easy to be a hero in someone else's
situation.

12. Intimacy
is joyous
and sad.

It is sharing,
open-ended, and
taking your mind off yourself
momentarily.

13. Money can't buy happiness, but it can
buy almost everything else.

14. Love is where it's at
and that's a fact.
(A refrain from a not-yet-composed
popular song.)

15. If hate doesn't become you, don't let it
come to be you.

16. If you've done something wrong, ask the
person you've wronged to forgive you.

17. The secret of being productive and
energetic is deciding (when you are up to it)

the parts of you that will remain
unchanged,
the aspects of your life that are not
important to change right now,

the things you don't feel like doing,
and then do, with vigor and dispatch, the
    one thing you want to do or must do
and then the next thing. When that's
    done, you'll have the time and
energy to do almost everything else you
    want to do.

It works almost every time.

18. Vibrations are real.

WHO DO YOU THINK YOU ARE SECTION

Nobody can be a hero in somebody else's situation.

FOR A SENSE OF YOURSELF

Look at yourself
    then ask a friend
how you are.
    If the two don't meet,
    retreat
for another look
at yourself.

I'M NOT A GURU, ARE YOU?

If you are
    searching for
the Answer
you won't find it here.

Make your own way to
the false messiahs,
true believers, and new charismatics
that abound
(to find you suggestable).

My way
is to raise questions
(tell stories)
about the nature of things
and the spirit of people.

The question is

if you feed the goldfish, how
do you expect them to express
their gratitude?

Or is it?

How can I find you
in the context of myself
and in the spirit of us all?

People who are
desperate about anything
   give off negative vibrations—

Like Peter,
   who desperately wants a girlfriend.
Like Sonia,
   who desperately wants her husband back.
Like John,
   who is desperately gregarious.
Like Candy,
   who desperately wants a man.
Like Rodney,
   who desperately wants sex.

Mind you—Peter, Sonia, John, Candy, and
especially Rodney are very nice people.
They just won't be satisfied with whatever
they get because the people they really want to
be close to are turned off by their desperation.

WHAT A PITY

Everyone has a story to tell.
Not everyone has someone to listen to it.

Everyone has a question to ask.
Not everyone feels free to ask it.

Everyone has something to give.
Not everyone knows how to go about it.

What a pity
we all can't be
Walter Mitty.

What a pity
    even Walter Mitty
when he "found himself"

    had to
        work,
    do his "homework,"
act the fool at times.

Ah, yes, life doesn't have to be a bore,
but it's no
    farghenigin*
        either.

* Yiddish for pleasure.

WHAT'S LIFE ALL ABOUT

Sometimes it takes
    a death of someone close—
an awareness,
    "there go I
    by the grace of God"
(I could have been gassed
in the holocaust),
a recovery from a terrible illness or accident,
    surviving a catastrophe
or a "simple" mugging

to discover how marvelous it is
    just to be alive
    with all our imperfections.

Some people are lucky.
    They know this without
    being reminded by tragedies.

THE LEGITIMACY
OF BEING UNHAPPY

Sometimes life is grim. There is nothing one can do except allow time to pass and heal. My own childhood was filled with years of a schooling I hated, a loneliness I didn't understand, and parents I didn't appreciate. I was unhappy but I didn't punish myself twice by ranting, raving, or projecting blame (yes, some tears and "woe is me," but not much). There are times when one must live with it, find relief in tears, and keep trusting the future. It is even common to contemplate suicide and imagine how sorry everybody will be. It's hard to resist the lure of irrational ways out.

My view is that it is worthwhile to think about relief from depression *before* it happens. Once you are in it, it's tough. The best solution for me is learning something new; for you it might be exercise.

There is nothing wrong with being unhappy every once in a while. There are many times and situations where unhappiness is the most appropriate response.

It's not hard to tell if your unhappiness has an important component of irrationality. The unhappiness comes with symptoms like

> fear of high or closed places;
> pains without disease, malfunctions,
>   or lesions;

chronic constipation;
gross loss of appetite;
sexual compulsions
that don't get you anyplace.

Rational unhappiness is dignified, unselfish, private, even a bit heroic. Unimpeded by irrational guilt or pride, it ends up being a learning experience.

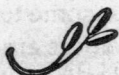

ON BEING PSEUDOTRUE

There are people who are so preoccupied with being independent that they are consumed by exaggerated fears of losing control over their own lives. Intimacy scares them because they see it as someone else's plan to manipulate or dominate them. Such people boast too much about expressing their true feelings, about being honest no matter what.

They lose out on the pleasures of caring. Their insensitivity causes pain to others. Their preoccupation with "being themselves" at all costs, their constant demands for acceptance "just as they are," cheat them out of the very thing they say they want most: to find their true selves. They are too busy with self-adulation and being selfish to risk the rewards of intimacy.

WHATEVER BECAME OF GUILT?

Guilt is a good thing to have if you've done something wrong. But there are two kinds.

Mature guilt helps you organize yourself, helps you respond in a more rational way the next time you face a similar situation or temptation. It enhances your self-esteem, provided you don't overdo it and let it degenerate into

immature guilt, which disorganizes and overwhelms a person. You can usually recognize it. Sometimes it stems from overreacting to something you did wrong. But more often the cause is something you did *not* do, or couldn't be responsible for or simply thought about. Immature guilt is a way of expressing anger at yourself. It leaves you feeling depressed, and you use these feelings of depression to get back at the other person. Immature guilt is triggered by an irrational aspect of your personality. Everyone, at one time or another, suffers the pain of immature guilt. Learning how to deal with it and how to solve the problems that cause it to happen can be important steps toward emotional growth and maturity.

Sometimes people come to me
and say,

"Life has no meaning."
They must go off and find themselves.

I reply,
"Where are you going? And
with whose money?"
You need to find yourself
where you are,
then go off and "find"
someone else to discuss *it*
with.

GOOD TIMES

I

If you've had a good
    time with someone
and the connection is broken

does that retrospectively
    spoil the
    good time?

What a pity
    and a travesty
to spoil
    something good from
the past
    for any reason.

II

If you've had good times
    with someone
and you discover that someone was not always
    faithful

does it spoil the good times?

I'm not possessive of anyone, so it spoils nothing
    for me.

III

Why regret anything you did for love?

EIGHTEEN "TRY NOT TO'S"
AND ONE "TRY HARD TO"

1. Try not to be a hero in someone else's situation.

2. Try not to use *the truth* as a way of expressing hostility.

3. Try not to boast.

4. Try not to be self-righteous.

5. Try not to tell more lies than you have to.

6. Try not to criticize others for defects you have yourself.

7. Try not to single out the most vulnerable aspect of someone else's life and talk good-naturedly about it.

8. Try not to be extra nice to people you don't like much—polite is good enough.

9. Try not to strive for perfection.

10. Try not to strive for humility.

11. Try not to identify with the lowest common denominator (peer pressure).

12. Try not to impress everyone (only someone).

13. Try not to say anything in a group if you can't say something positive.

14. Try not to love someone who can't or won't love back.

15. Try not to mind anyone else's business unless invited to.

16. Try not to tear yourself down or build yourself up on other people's account.

17. Try not to avoid constructive criticism.

18. Try not to overdo anything.

Try hard to stand for something.
Otherwise, you'll fall for anything.

DIFFERENTIAL RISKS

I don't know why grown
    people take dangerous risks (some of
    which are lethal).

Presumably normal people
    overeat,
    drink more than they should,
    race cars,
    gamble,
    smoke,
    speed,
    have sex without birth control,
    cheat (sometimes calling it private enterprise).

But if it's a teen-ager taking the
risk,
    watch out
for all the labels, interpretations,
and diagnostic categorizations
pasted
    or him or her.

WHAT'S DIFFICULT
IN LIFE FOR ALL OF US

I

Not to take a foolish risk
As well as to acknowledge afterwards
That it wasn't worth it after all.

II

To purge your fantasy
Of a miracle happening to you
As well as to settle for the fact that unless you
Work for what you want
Nothing much will happen at all.

III

To give up the feeling that you are not lucky
But that so many other people you know are.

IV

To give up the possibility of romantic love lasting
     forever—
The ultimate fantasy of all of us.

THINGS ALMOST ALL PEOPLE DO OR THINK ABOUT SOMETIMES BUT DO NOT OFTEN WANT TO ACKNOWLEDGE

Embellish stories they tell.

Want to make others laugh.

Feel sorry for themselves.

Tell lies.

Want to be rich.

Slight others without realizing it.

Have weird dreams.

Think they must be losing their minds.

Forget important dates like birthdays and anniversaries.

Are depressed every once in a while.

Masturbate.

Wonder if they did the right thing by marrying, going to college, having children, etc.

Are turned on sexually by parts of strangers or animals.

Have sexual or murderous thoughts about people they love or hate.

Cheer for the underdog.

Are cruel for unexplained reasons or in unexpected circumstances.

Doubt the existence of God.

Are aware of the mean part of themselves.

BOREDOM SECTION

If you are bored,
you are boring to be with.

So if you are bored, don't
tell anyone,
        but here are eighteen things
you can do by yourself,
        and if one of them "works"
then find someone
to spend time with.

1. Write a letter to someone who would be
   surprised to hear from you.

2. Give yourself a massage.

3. Write a haiku (a seventeen-syllable poem
   arranged in three lines of five, seven, and five
   syllables).

4. Go to a park, a museum, or a play—something
   you would *never* think of doing on your own.

5. Find five words in a dictionary that you've
   heard of but don't know the meanings of, and
   study them until you do.

6. Munch a raw carrot very slowly.

7. Watch a program on TV that you wouldn't
   ordinarily watch—maybe a documentary
   on PBS.

8. Go see a *serious* movie.

9. Purchase a magazine that you wouldn't
   ordinarily read—*Playgirl, New Republic, The
   Humanist, Ms., Family Circle, Rolling Stone,*

Forum, or *Seventeen*—and read at least two articles in it.

10. Discover the radio. Don't watch TV for a whole day (a whole week would be better). Find out what radio has to offer *aside from* your favorite music.

11. Be your own psychodrama. Act out a *scene* for at least twenty minutes that you would like to play in real life. Be very animated and enthusiastic.

12. Bake bread or cookies from scratch.

13. Take a warm bath.

14. Write down all the things you really like to do. Don't stop until you've written down at least as many as your age. If you are twenty years old you should be able to write twenty things you really enjoy—and add at least one to the list every year. Then without giving it much thought, *do* one of the things on your list.

15. Go shopping and buy something for yourself —spend a little more than you can afford.

16. Daydream without feeling guilty.

17. Fix or build something.

18. If nothing else works, try exercise.

Now, call up a friend and ask what's new. If the friend says nothing is new, hang up right away and call someone else.

When you are bored
the following steps to relieve same
won't work
(for more than a few minutes).

alcohol
pills of any sort
TV—the more you watch the more bored you
        become
feeling sorry for yourself
eating
sleeping
anger
neglecting your personal appearance (I might as
        well look as rotten bored as I feel)
complaining
gambling
feeling guilty
reckless spending
driving fast
sex with anyone you don't know or care about
procrastinating
breaking things (you just have to pick up the
        pieces)
denial
telling everybody that you are bored, Bored,
        BORED

LINES FOR BORING
CONVERSATIONS

Nobody understands me.

Why me?

If it rains it pours.

This is not my day.

That's the way it goes.

That's life.

I hate to say it, but I told you so.

I couldn't care less.

Who's to say?

If it's not up, it's down.

Why pick on me?

How come you're not on my side?

I don't know how you keep up this pace.

If one more thing happens, I'm going to climb the
    walls.

Oh God, not again.

I can't believe this is happening to me again.

I'll never make it through the day.

This weather would get anyone down.

I can really dig your silence.

I know it's none of my business but . . .

Let's get together one of these days.

WORRY
AND
DEPRESSION
SECTION

If it isn't one thing,
it's another.

WORRYING IS GOOD FOR YOU
SOMETIMES

I get fed up with people who tell me not to worry,
especially doctors who use it as an excuse not to
tell me what I am entitled to know, and
self-centered busybodies and know-nothings who
think that my worries don't amount to much
because only their own worries are the *real ones*.

    People like that are always telling me:
        You have nothing to worry about.
        You call that something to worry about?
        That should be your worst worry.
        So, what's the worry?
        Worrying doesn't help.
        It doesn't pay to worry.
        Worrying isn't good for you.
        Don't worry. It'll all work out in the end.
        Is that all you've got to worry about?
        My dear, let me tell you about real worries.

    Sometimes I use a lot of relatively
unimportant worries to block out temporarily big,
important worries that I can't do anything about.
It's very helpful to me to do that—even though
intellectually I realize that it would be better to do
something constructive.

    But sometimes I don't have the peace of mind
        or the will or the energy and that's all
        right too.
    And sometimes worrying is the background

or even the inspiration for a creative idea that I can write down, even after a restless night.

If one really good thought or plan emerges, it would be worth it after all.

The best worrying leads to some action and resolution. But it's very difficult to turn off real worries (as I think about it, all worries are real). Worrying becomes destructive when it interferes with everything else you want to do, when it's used as a weapon against other people, and when it's repressed and turns into symptoms.

I worry a lot because I have a lot to worry about. I don't want no worrywart telling me not to worry. I worry a lot and I get a lot done too.

DEPRESSED?

What should I do
when I am depressed?

Learn something new.

What do I often do
when I am depressed?

I eat too much, worry a
lot, pace up and down,
and don't get a damn
thing done.

What else could I do?

Go out for a walk, listen
to music, call up a friend,
go to a good movie.

What do I often do?

Watch TV.
Buy a painting I can't
afford.
See a rotten movie.
Read useless books.

(I don't often drink
alcohol
when I'm depressed—
it makes me feel worse
afterwards.)

What works best?

I learn something new.
I teach someone
something new.
And, if worse comes to
worse, I go on a big trip.

USES AND ABUSES
OF OUR PAST

The past
is for
delicious memories,
nostalgia,
learning from,
and forgetting,

not for
torture,
feeling stuck in,
or remembering
everything.

DEPRESSED

I have friends,
a wife who cares
for me,
and I her;
I have money,
a beautiful home
with paintings, books, music,
a wood-burning fireplace,
and a cleaning lady once a week.
I'm sort of famous.

So why am I not satisfied?

THOUGHTS
WHEN I'M DEPRESSED

I

Nobody is happy.
   Nobody?
Are you happy?
I suppose there are happy people
but I don't know anyone who is.

II

I'm depressed.
Are you really?
Yes.
Isn't everybody these days?
At least everybody I know is.

III

Time to think?
  Spare me.
Time to think?
  My last resort.
Time to think?
  I've thought all the thoughts
  I want to think.

Now I need time for poetry.

Time to think
  depresses me
  instantly.

LIVING
LIVELY
SECTION

Don't give me that old song and dance.
Give me another one.

Make friends (lovers come and go).
Learn one thing well.
Collect something.
Develop a new passion (each year).
Listen to music (carefully).
Daydream (a lot).
Engage in animated conversations.
Support a cause.
Laugh (if it's funny).
Don't watch TV (that much).
Exercise.
Don't crash diet (but stop junk foods).
Write letters.
No smoking (please).
Enjoy nature.
Travel.
Read a daily newspaper,
    two weekly magazines,
    four monthly ones,
    fiction (my current favorite is John Irving).
Try walking.
Be nice to someone each day,
    to someone most people are not nice to,
    to at least one parent for at least one moment
        every once in a while without being asked.
Be (what you think is) yourself part of each day.
Sit in a chair for five minutes (every day) and
don't do anything.
Fall in and out of love
 until you want to marry and then

stay in love as long as you can (to the person
you marry).
Attend at least one opera,
                        ballet,
                        play,
                        circus,
                        lecture,
                        concert,
                        art show,
and then shout for joy at making a new discovery.
Be sexually active only with someone you care
about.
If you are not able to earn the amount of money
you want (just yet) at least earn the respect you
need now.
An ultimate high: gaining the respect of the
people you care about.
The ultimate low: losing one's self-respect.

CARRY ON AS THOUGH
THERE IS A TOMORROW.

ON BECOMING A
SELF-FULFILLED PROPHECY

If you feel unattractive
    It becomes you.

If you feel friendless
    It becomes you.

People become what they feel
No matter how
    Attractive or friendly
    They appear to be.

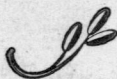

RELATIONSHIPS

Relationships
    born out of desperation
    seldom
      last
longer than relationships
    fashioned out of despair.
Relationships
    kindled by needs
are rarely fired by passion or desire.

If I need you
    (for some reason or other)
Or if you need me
    (et cetera)

It often becomes a mismatch of
    different,
    changing,
    faltering,
    disintegrating
emotions.
But if we want
    each other
We stand a chance
because people who want each other
    leave room for
    disappointments,
    privacy, and
    peak periods of passion.

I like repeating myself over and over again.
> That part of my life is security.

I like new experiences.
> That part of my life is adventure.

I like being open to love.
> That part of my life is sensual.

I like books, music, art, 'n' stuff.
> That part of my life is aesthetic.

Everything else is boring.
> That part of my life is supposed to be relevant.

REALITY
SECTION

So far so good.*

* The Gordon battle cry.

TESTING

Everything must be
tested
in relation to
another human.

Every human is tested
in relationships.

Without relationships
everything is a test.

HAVE YOU NOTICED

that outside of
your
very best,
    closest,
really intimate friends,

no one is interested
in your troubles,
except, of course,
a few wretched gossips
who thrive on them.

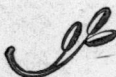

RELATIVITY

Everything is relative
     and has its limitations,
     except
your fantasies.

Limitations are relative,
     except
     your fantasies,
which are limitless.

DISAPPOINTMENTS

I

Expectations are
usually
better
than the real thing;
if it turns out
otherwise,
enjoy,
but don't expect it
to happen again
soon.

II

Anticipations are
invariably
more exciting
than what happens;

If the
real thing
comes even remotely
close,
live with it.

III

Disappointments
are part of
living.

SOMETIMES I FEEL ALONE
BUT IT DOES NOT LAST LONG

Does one ever
    recapture
a flight of fancy,
a past passion,
a lost regret?

Can one ever
fall in love
in retrospect?

The present fire
offers a warm glow;

The past fire
a bittersweet memory.

ALAS—ONE AND TWO

Sometimes the best one can do
    isn't good enough
To change a situation
    at all.

        If you are angry
            or having an argument,
        Stop after two minutes
            and say to yourself,
        Whose problem is it?

LOVE
SECTION

*Love is blind only for people
who blunder into it.*

FIVE HOW CAN YOU TELLS

How can you tell if you are *really* in love?

Mature love is energizing. You have enough time and energy for most of the things you want to do. When you are with your lover, you feel happy, elevated, and secure.

Immature love is exhausting. You feel tired and incapacitated most of the time. When you are with your lover, you spend the time fighting and arguing. You feel inferior and insecure.

To learn more about love, try falling in and out of it, and analyze what you learn as you go. Read at least two books about it, like *The Heart of Loving* by Eugene Kennedy and *The Art of Loving* by Erich Fromm, and then set about the business of discovering all the other things that may be missing from your life.

How can you tell if a person is handing you a line?

Very easy. That person will want to test you by making sex a condition of the relationship.

How can you tell if a particular behavior is normal?

Normal behavior tends to be voluntary, nonexploitive, and self-limiting. You choose when to do it, you don't hurt anyone else, and you stop when you're ready.

Abnormal behavior tends to be involuntary. You cannot seem to control it. It is repetitive, guilt-ridden, and harmful to yourself and to others.

How can you tell the difference between falling in love and falling for lust?

People sometimes mistake sexual arousal for love. Caring deeply for another person is something quite apart from being "turned on" by anatomy: tits, an ankle, a bicep, an erect penis. Love has a great deal to do with being able to talk, but you can't have a conversation with an ass, not even a smart one.

Good sex is possible between partners who hardly know each other or who hate each other. But no matter how good the sex is, it can never turn hate into love or take the place of caring and conversation. Less than adequate sex is possible between partners who know each other very well and love each other very much. Their sex lives can become better with effort and perhaps help.

How can you tell whom not to marry?

Don't marry anyone who keeps asking, "Do you love me, do you really love me?" (If you are smart, you will say no. Then you will probably have your first real conversation.)

Don't marry anyone who makes promises about the future. (After we're married, I'll stop drinking. After the baby is born, I'll stop working so late every night.) Test these resolutions *before* marriage and children. It is very doubtful that someone who can't break a rotten habit today will be able to give it up later when the calendar says it's time.

Don't marry anyone who is more devoted to television, work, sports, money, bars, or housecleaning than to you.

Don't marry anyone who lacks a sense of humor.

Don't marry anyone who doesn't respect your intelligence. (Don't marry ANYONE until YOU respect your own intelligence.)

Don't marry anyone out of desperation. Some people are so desperate to marry that they forget to notice whether they are loved in return. Don't confuse loving with being loved. These are two separate and basic needs. One is no substitute for the other.

A SYMPHONY OF LOVE
NOT ALWAYS RECIPROCATED
(in four erratic movements)

Prologue

Love without
lust
is dull;
without
passion,
boring;
but without
friendship,
a disaster.

I

You came to me
with a vision,
touching with your eyes
and mind.

And when you
touched me
it was without
passion.

Struggling for meaning,

you could
only embrace the body
of my intellect.

Yet
    how I prefer this pain
to nothingness
the morning after
lust alone.

Later
    we talked about God
and energy.

But only later, much later,
when we experienced
love,
did
God and energy
seem worth talking about.

II

Each of us
on a separate
journey
loves
the other

without passion
or regret,
toward a vision
of God's message
of despair
and reconciliation.

Leave it be,
my dearest,
leave it be.

III

When two people find each other
they go on a journey
to discover all the other "things"
that are missing in their lives.

IV

Why can't we still be friends?
I can't handle it, that's way,
    she replied,
and we never saw each other again.

THREE VERSIONS OF
EIGHTEEN VARIETIES OF LOVE

I

Longing for Heritage

After I've done the best I can,
I feel something is missing.

I miss
not having traditions
in my life (any longer),
even the Friday sabbath
dinners.

Form and rituals,
however boring,
offer a sense
of security and continuity.

I wonder
sometimes
if I will become
religious
out of despair
or insecurity
however much

I want to embrace
God
out of love.

II
Before Intimacy

Joys can be shared
(Suffering is mainly personal),
Love energizing,
Hate exhausting.

Optimism is contagious,
Pessimism debilitating.

Envy, greed, jealousy, and
prejudice are connected to
self-deprecation,
while
admiration, affirmation, and
caring for others to self-esteem.

Why live in the past
if your future is in the present?

No one can make you
feel
inferior without your
consent.

80

Love Can Afford to
Be Blind Only on the
First Day of It

Our brief encounters
that one day by chance
touched me more
than instant intimacy
the night before
with someone
more enthusiastic.

Our unscheduled interludes,
rising and descending
in meaning and intensity,
thrusting close to love,
failed to inspire trust
(I'm glad to say),
left you afraid, excited, worried
before risking anything
you would regret.

Why did you happen to be
so dear to me?

Who needs you anyway?
There is always someone else

(I'm not insecure).
I can get along without you,
to be sure.
But why should I?
Should I?

IF YOU REALLY LOVE ME
YOU'LL HAVE SEX WITH ME

If anyone says that to you,
you can be sure it's a line.*
Sex cannot be, by itself,
a proof of love—Usually
it's a ploy to have sex and run.

Here are some lines and some "good"
responses that are *yours* to use
—until such time as people stop
playing with each other.

Male (at the drive-in): Would you like to get into
   the back seat?
Female: No. I'd rather sit up here with you.

Male: I think you're different.
Female: So do I.

Male: Come on, try me. I'll be the best you've
   ever had.
Female: No matter how hard you try, you could
   never be good enough for me.

Male: If you don't stay over you'll never know
   what you're missing.
Female: Yes, I do; that's why the answer is NO!

* See my book *You would if you loved me*, published in
paperback by Bantam.

Male: This night has been one of the best. You've really been a lot of fun. I've never met anyone like you. I'll bet you're just as much fun in bed too, aren't you?

Female: Yes, I'm dynamite, but I'm definitely not set to go off with you.

Male: I think we could make great rhythm.

Female: Sorry, but I don't dance.

Male: Don't worry. I'll use protection.

Female: You're going to need protection if you don't leave me alone.

Male: Do you want to watch the sun rise in the morning?

Female: Just the sun.

EVEN LOVE

Really meaningful experiences in life
have peaks
    of brief duration
which are repeatable.
    Even love
    is
    imperfect,
leaves us open
    to be
        hurt,
        vulnerable,
        misunderstood,
yet
leaves room for
    growth,
    excitement,
    joy,
becoming more ourselves
    by offering more to the other,
but that doesn't mean
    that our timing is always right
even when we love each other.

THE
SEX
SECTION

Remember the "good old days"?
Remember when the air was clean
and sex was dirty?

INTRODUCTION

People who feel good about themselves and see life as worthwhile and an opportunity for new and exciting experiences are not candidates for sexual exploitation. People whose sense of worth depends on having someone else love them or who feel useless in the absence of love find it difficult to look beyond expressions and declarations of passion undying to see whether they are being used.

I subscribe to the definition developed by the World Health Organization* that sex education should be "far more broadly and imaginatively conceived" to deal not only with reproductive physiology but with "questions of ethics in interpersonal relationships and responsibility in reproductive behavior." The intent of sexuality education—as described and interpreted by one of the world's most distinguished pioneers in the field, Dr. Mary Calderone (president of the Sex Education and Information Council of the United States)—is the development of mature individuals who are capable of making wise and responsible decisions in the fulfillment of their sexual lives. The best sex education always explores the moral values underlying all relationships.

* World Health Organization, *Education and Treatment In Human Sexuality: The Training of Health Professionals* (Washington, D.C.: WHO Publications, 1975).

EIGHTEEN FACTS AND
IDEAS I CONSIDER AMONG
THE MOST IMPORTANT

1. On Being Sexually Attractive

People who accept themselves are sexually attractive to *some* other people. It's not that short, fat, or "unattractive" people can't "find" a mate—it's that people who hate themselves and express it by unattractive *behavior,* by being shortsighted or fatuous, tend to repel others. Believing that certain perfumes, hair tonics, vaginal sprays, or sexual techniques or postures will make you "attractive" will get you nowhere.

It doesn't matter what the cosmetic and toothpaste industries have to say about it. No deodorant can be a substitute for self-acceptance. What really attracts other good people is *being* a good person.

2. Sexual Arousal

The popular culture, and especially its mass media, creates the notion of standard stimuli for sexual arousal. Men are "supposed" to be excited by pictures of pretty girls selling automobiles or by Playboy bunnies. There is nothing inherently wrong with this kind of thinking, except that people who aren't aroused by the current fashion often feel obliged to fake it.

The fact is that human beings are sexually excited by an endless variety of stimuli. Some people become sexually aroused when playing with children, roughhousing with dogs, sitting in cars, fantasizing about danger. And some people like pornography, although I find it boring because my own mind is a lot more explicit than anything a pornographer can put down on paper. But to say that pornography is harmful is misleading. Research does not support this view. If anything, pornography inhibits overt sexual behavior. For many people, including myself, the ultimate arousal is getting to know somebody.

A problem may develop if you are excited only by thoughts or acts that you or your partner cannot accept.

If you can accept feelings of arousal without guilt, no harm is done. In fact, why not enjoy it?

3. Select—Don't Settle

Human beings are not animals. Animal sex is biologically programmed—but even animals, if the opposite sex is not available, "make do" with their own. At this stage of our evolution it seems that human sexuality is not fixed. People can go through stages, mistakes, incidents, encounters, affairs at different times of their lives that can include long and short periods of fidelity and infidelity, homosexual liaisons, brief associations, weird indiscretions, or a "perversion" here and there. People can grow and profit from experience.

It's all right to feel that you are naturally attracted only to members of the opposite sex (for whatever reason and no matter how open or modern you think you are). But for many people other possibilities and attractions are boundless. With as little as we know about sexual preferences, it does appear that no sensible person need worry that heterosexuality will disappear as a primary sex style. The real concern in most of the world is overpopulation, not whether more people are a-, bi-, auto-, or homosexual—or simply don't want children.

Not everything in life is natural, harmonious, congruous, or logical. Not everything fits. This is why we must at least try to select what we want most of all without settling for what can only be our despair. I don't mean to select one thing and be done with it. What makes sense in one period of life may make no sense during another. In any case, most of what we do most of the time will not be a gourmet experience.

4. All Thoughts Are Normal

Sexual thoughts, wishes, dreams, daydreams are normal—no matter how far out. Behavior can be wrong but ideas cannot. Anybody with the slightest bit of imagination has, from time to time, had murderous, sadistic, incestuous, or rape fantasies. That does not mean they are going to act them out. The people who severely repress their fantasies or become preoccupied with guilt over them are most likely to cause harm to themselves and to others.

Guilt is the energy for the repetition of unacceptable thoughts. The best way of keeping "unacceptable" thoughts under control is to accept them as normal. Let me give a few examples:

I walk down the street and notice a woman who captures my fancy. I have sex with her. The woman doesn't know about it. My wife doesn't know about it. I don't feel guilty. And I have a very enjoyable walk.

A fifteen-year-old boy caught a glimpse of his thirteen-year-old sister taking a shower. His first thought was to have sex with her. He felt terribly guilty and could not free his mind of the image or the sexual wish. Nobody in his family could understand why he began to avoid his friends, became hostile toward his sister, and seemed to be getting more and more depressed.

In this case, guilt caused the fantasy to return over and over again. It became obsessive and the boy was preoccupied with it. After a while he might forget or repress the incident and only hostility toward the sister would remain. What a pity he didn't understand that his thought was normal. Had he known, the thought would have remained with him briefly—whether he enjoyed it or not doesn't matter—and nothing would have happened.

5. *Examples of Immature or Neurotic Sex*

Compulsive masturbation. You do it not because you like it but because you can't help it. Perhaps you are punishing yourself to satisfy guilt feelings.

Compulsive heterosexual or homosexual behavior (even if not forced upon the other person). The behavior takes place outside an interest in a relationship. It does not enhance or enrich the person and it rarely provides gratification beyond momentary relief. For instance, a person who is always "on the make" is rarely capable of a sustained relationship and, despite "boasting" to the contrary, usually does not enjoy sex.

Other examples of immature behavior:

Being talked into having sex when you really don't want to, before you feel ready for it, with someone you don't really care about, or without using birth control (unless, of course, you *both* want and will take care of a child).

When your main thing (in order to achieve some sexual outlet) is a thing (shoe, undergarment, dress) or when other forms of indirect behavior such as exposing yourself, stealing, or viewing others (Peeping Tom) becomes a compulsive behavior.

6. *Masturbation*

Nearly everyone these days says that masturbation is all right . . . a normal developmental stage . . . and then there is a pause. "It's all right if you don't do it too much." And nearly everyone is asking the question "How much is too much?" Once a year? Twice a month? After every meal?

The answer: Once is too much if you don't enjoy it.

In my day, it was simple. No question about it. From "playing with yourself" you got acne, tired blood, insanity, and blindness (that's why I wear glasses). We were pioneers in those days!

Masturbation is a normal sexual expression for all people, no matter at what age or stage in life you happen to be—child, teen-ager, young adult, middle-aged, elderly, single, or married.

Masturbation is best when it is voluntary (as opposed to compulsive) and it is accompanied by a wide range of fantasies. (Why not pick the most exciting?)

There is no physical harm no matter how frequently men or women masturbate. Nor is the sperm supply affected by frequency of masturbation.

A wet dream (nocturnal emission in males) and orgasm stimulated by dreams in women is mental masturbation and is as natural as using the hand.

The idea that people who masturbate "a lot" don't make friends or are "selfish" is just plain silly. (How long does it take to masturbate? Why should it interfere with making friends?)

Compulsive eating, talking, sleeping, and masturbating are examples of "natural" behavior that can be symptomatic of "problems." This does not make eating, talking, sleeping, and masturbating "unnatural." If I had to "settle" for one compulsive behavior to express my "problems" I would certainly "select" masturbation.

A lot of people don't often admit it, but they achieve their "best" orgasms by masturbating. A lot of married people with satisfactory sex lives masturbate. Some people (not many) masturbate hardly at all or not at all. That's all right too. Guilt about masturbation is about the only thing that's bad about it.

7. Penis Size

Myth: Penis envy is a woman's problem.

Revision: The only people I know with penis envy are men. It's an all-American hang-up! Men worry if theirs is BIG enough. Most at some time in their lives (or often) have looked around in public bathrooms or showers to see if they could find one smaller than their own.

Facts:

1. Penis size has nothing to do with giving or receiving sexual pleasure.

2. You cannot tell the size of a penis by looking at it when it is not erect. Some hang long; others you can hardly see. Some of those that appear quite small erect to sizes larger than those that appear huge.

3. Women needlessly worry that their partner's penis is either too small for satisfaction or too big ("painful") for their "small" vagina. When we recall that the vagina accommodates the birth of a baby, it is not difficult to appreciate

that genital size itself is not the factor in pleasure or pain.

Breast Size

Breast size (or shape) has nothing to do with sexual or personal adequacy. In the early stages of puberty, girls often worry because of uneven or "late" breast development (compared to their friends). This is sad because there is a wide range of perfectly healthy, normal stages of growth. With so many real things to worry about, why worry about something that represents a natural process that takes its own time?

Many girls with "large" breasts are as self-conscious as those with small ones. The "style" shifts from the larger the better to the smaller the better. *Don't* let "style" mess you up (surgical alterations can be very dangerous). Besides, breast size has nothing to do with sexual responsiveness.

8. *First Experiences of Sexual Intercourse*

Note: Every new person you have sex with is a *first experience*.

Many first experiences of sex are not pleasurable, despite stories to the contrary. This is especially so when they occur when you are too young, too immature, or on your honeymoon. Some men think they are sexual freaks if they are impotent or ejaculate prematurely, while some women feel that they are not sexual or feminine if they don't have an orgasm the first time around.

It is especially important not to diagnose yourself on the basis of these experiences. Sex becomes enjoyable for two people who are sensitive to each other.

Sex can become a nightmare, empty, flat, even repulsive if the partners don't care about each other, concentrate on position games and simultaneous orgasms, or must sneak, hide, and hurry.

However, it *is* possible to be sexually functional with someone (even a spouse) you don't care about.

It *is* also possible to love and care about someone (even a spouse) with whom you are or become sexually dysfunctional (e.g., impotent or nonorgasmic). The problem could have originated before you knew your partner. Don't panic. More likely than not it is temporary. It could be due to guilt, a recent trauma, inexperience, or unfavorable conditions often associated with the first sexual experiences. It could be the result of mutual and naive insensitivity. Sexual difficulties of this kind are usually solved when two people work at their problems with empathy and mutual understanding.

9. *Prevention of Sex Problems*
First, be well informed. (Even if you think you know it all, start by reading some of the books recommended at the end of this section.)

Second, learn to become sensual. Discover your own body. Find out the parts of your body that are most erotic.

Try this from time to time:

Lie naked on the bed. Close your eyes and slowly caress every part of your body. Open your eyes and stimulate and caress every part of your body, including your genitals and anus. (If you are ticklish whenever anybody touches you, it can mean you are afraid of being sensual. Repeat this method to reduce your sensitivity to being tickled in order to become more sensual.)

Don't be afraid to masturbate if you feel like it. Enjoy your fantasies at the same time.

Let your shower or bath become a sensual experience.

Feeling sexual is a good feeling.

10. *If You Have a Sexual Intercourse Problem* or you are nervous about new sex experiences:

Concentrate on the relationship. Talk about areas of concern and mutual pleasure. Do active things together (almost anything except watching TV).

Hold off having sexual intercourse. Get to know each other's bodies. Give each other a bath. Massage each other (lots of good "how-to" books on the market, but let your partner tell you what feels the best). Masturbate each other. Use other orifices.

And when you feel ready try intercourse, but without concern about the orgasm.

Give it some months if you are living together, longer if you are not always together. And if it doesn't work, seek professional help.

11. *For People Who Think They Want to Be Unliberated*

You can't use another person to validate who you are. Only if you are fulfilled yourself can you have a fulfilling relationship with another person.

Which is not to say that some people don't adjust well to unliberated relationships (à la Total Woman), but if you develop symptoms (depressions, frequent headaches, and anxiety attacks, reconsider . . .

On Giving Up One's Career Goals in Order to Support Your Mate's Getting His or Hers

One alternative is to work out a contract: After s/he finishes, you are next.

Many people (mostly women) work their fingers to the bone (as secretaries, of course) to enable their husbands to complete their under- or postgraduate studies, only then to be abandoned and "exchanged" for a woman with a comparable degree.

12. *Virgin Rights*

It is safe to assume that if about 70 percent of women who marry have sex before marriage, then about 30 percent wait until marriage. And notwithstanding the figure for males who wait (about 15 percent), we must emphatically declare that virgins have rights too. Despite massive societal support for virgins, this group is rapidly becoming more maligned and more vulnerable.

Of course, there are no "pressures" for virgins to organize to protect their rights. Can you imagine an organization called the Virgin Activist League, with the slogan, "Power to the Virgins," and a button, "Virginity is Beautiful"?

Now I happen to believe that committed virgins should stick to their guns and not be intimidated by peer pressure. Our society, for its very survival, needs more people who have the courage of their convictions. Just because some of the worst elements in the Establishment support (often for people other than themselves) the virginal state is no reason to question its validity. Some of society's best people also support virginity.

It is no accident that in my twenty-five years as a practicing psychologist, no young person has ever asked my consent for sex—yet I am frequently asked if it is normal to wait until marriage. I, of course, reply, "Yes." I could be very sanctimonious and stop there, but I add: "If you are going to wait, I trust that you won't expect simultaneous orgasms on your wedding night. Otherwise you might ask yourself the question 'For this I waited?' "*

Sometimes, a young man will say to me, "I want to marry a virgin." I reply, "I hope you'll marry a person, not a hymen."

13. *Gay*
It is no longer believed that homosexuality is

---

* "For this I waited?" is an effective comment only when said with a Jewish accent.

caused by any one thing or special combination of factors. The only thing we are reasonably sure of is that homosexuals were brought up by heterosexual couples. Homosexuals exist in every culture and society. The ancient Greek culture found homosexuality acceptable. Our culture frowns upon it. In any case, we now know that homosexual experiences are not rare during childhood and adolescence. These experiences do not necessarily mean that a person will become an adult homosexual. Many young people who have had more than just a few homosexual experiences have been known to marry successfully. It is *untrue* that if you have homosexual thoughts or dreams, you must be a homosexual. Mature people are aware of the fact that they have both homosexual and heterosexual feelings, even though the majority of them prefer sexual activities with members of the opposite sex. In this connection you should know that it is not easy to judge whether a person is a homosexual. Some feminine-looking men or masculine-looking women are heterosexual and some highly "masculine," muscular, so-called all-American types of men are homosexual.

As far as we know now, homosexuality is not hereditary, biological, chemical, or constitutional. It is not known why a person selects a homosexual life-style any more than it is known in any particular case why a person opts for heterosexuality. I would suspect that few people would be exclusively one way or another if we

102

were more open about our sexual attractions. Men in our society are especially frightened by normal desires for intimacy with another male because of their fear of being diagnosed as homosexual.

A sensible "definition" of a homosexual is a person who, in his or her adult life, prefers and has sexual relations almost exclusively with members of the same sex. Saying a person is a homosexual tells us as much about the person as saying a person is heterosexual. If we're going to sex-identify each other, let's start out with the idea that we are all human sexuals. There is no such thing as latent homosexuality in the sense that it is, by itself, a problem. Everyone starts out with latent bi-, homo-, auto-, and heterosexualities. People who are afraid of their healthy sexual impulses have a problem no matter what expression it takes.

People should be free, without stigma or coercion, to lead the sexual life that's "right" for them. If some 85 percent "choose" heterosexuality, that's their business. If perhaps 15 percent choose homosexuality, bisexuality, or celibacy, that's their business. Certainly it is cruel and immoral for the state to have anything to say about sexual relations between two consenting adults.

The gay liberation movement has made it abundantly clear that homosexuals are, in fact, just as healthy or unhealthy as heterosexuals. Sexual preference does not determine whether a person is mature or "normal."

14. *Coitus*

Many myths are perpetuated by sexperts who write sex manuals and the "everything you want to know" kind of trash.

Most important!

There is no special amount of time a man's penis is supposed to stay in a woman's vagina in order to guarantee satisfaction. For some, it's a few seconds; for others, a couple of minutes (and *it* can vary from time to time and each time, as a matter of fact). The presumed norm of fifteen minutes is ridiculous. Most couples find this amount of time a crushing bore (some, of course, like it sometimes).

There are no standards for everyone or even most everyone (even if I imply it). Find out by experimenting what is most enjoyable for you and your partner.

Next

Penis–vagina intercourse is not essential for sexual pleasure—nor is having an orgasm each time or any time, and certainly not having simultaneous orgasm. Mutual stimulation and/or masturbation (many women achieve orgasm only through masturbation or by having someone stimulate them clitorally) are alternatives, although some women cannot tolerate the direct stimulation of their clitoris.

There are many ways couples can enjoy sex— oral, anal, titular, and massage. Experiment!

The largest number of uptight people are found among the rigid heterosexuals who each time must get in and do "it" only one way (missionary).

Any relentlessly fixed sexuality (be it in a hetero- or homosexual context) is probably unhealthy or at best unimaginative.

15. *Female Orgasm—Male Orgasm*

More nonsense has been written about this subject than about any other area of sexuality. Women have been made to feel so insecure about so many things that some need a Good Housekeeping Seal to certify their orgasms.

Often they pose the question in a serious way to a professional: "How can I tell if I have an orgasm?" And just as often the professional will respond with an idiotic answer like "If you had one, you'd know it." This response only reinforces the insecurity. Some women have orgasm without being sure about it.

Orgasm is essentially a psychological phenomenon—with physical sensations associated with it.* Orgasm is not always necessary in order to enjoy sexual intimacy and a full mature relationship with another human being. It's just another dimension of pleasure that is good to experience.

Most women who enjoy their own bodies, have good feelings about themselves, and like the idea of sexual intimacy have orgasms:

---

* We define orgasm as a very brief, intensely pleasurable sensual experience often associated with a series of "contractions."

If they are not intent on having one each time.

If their partner doesn't ask, "Did you have one?" each time. (What kind of conversation is that anyway?)

If they don't take seriously some of the silly research, especially the kind that suggests what kind of father you should have had in order to get one.

And/or if they masturbate.

The Myth of the Male Orgasm

The best kept male secret is the myth that every time a man ejaculates, he has an orgasm. This is simply not true and any man who denies it is either not telling the truth or can't be trusted.

Sometimes a man will ejaculate and feel nothing at all. At times there is a little pleasure and at times a great deal. Orgasms vary in strength and pleasure. I suspect that men fake orgasms as much as women do. The male orgasm is just as much a psychological phenomenon as female orgasm.

16. *Sex at a Young Age*

(another way of saying adolescent sex)

Most young people will have had a few, or many, "sexual intercourses" during their adolescence. When young people have sex they don't ask for their parents' consent. They know that their parents will say no. Teen-agers also don't ask me or any other counselors, because we all have a tendency to say no! But adolescents don't listen to us. So, I quickly add, "Look, if you are not going to pay attention to me, at least use birth control."

The main problem is that *most* young people experimenting with their first intercourse do not use birth control.* Many girls think it is unromantic to be prepared. Irresponsible boys feel it's the girl's job to worry about it. Not very smart girls fall for lines like "Don't worry about it, I'll pull out in time" or "I don't get any feeling when I use a rubber [condom]" or "It's too expensive." Girls should respond, "What about my feelings when I'm pregnant, need an abortion, or give birth?" or "If you're too cheap to spend thirty-five cents for a rubber, then you *can't come in.*"

There are other problems when young, immature people have sex. The first experiences, often due to unfortunate circumstances and/or lack of knowledge, tend to be disappointing or without pleasure and are often misinterpreted by the people involved to mean that there must be something wrong with them.

Many adults who have consulted therapists because of sexual problems have been able to trace them to traumatic sexual experiences during their adolescence. Of course, many people also can recall that their only really good love and

* For the last several years the birth rate has been rising among teen-agers but declining in every other age group, even among the traditional high birthrate groups—the poor, blacks, and Catholics.

sexual experiences took place in their teen years.

So the best I can say to young people is if you want sex, it's better to wait until you are older (in college or working), but if you are going to anyway—use birth control and join the campaign against absurd state laws that prohibit teen-agers from securing birth control information and services without parental consent.

17. *A Few Basic Facts About Some Sexually Transmitted Diseases (STD): Syphilis, Gonorrhea, and Herpes Genitalis*

Sexually transmitted diseases are caused by germs spread by hetero- or homosexual contact (including the genitals, mouth, and anus).

Syphilis can attack any part of the body.

Untreated syphilis can cause sterility, blindness, insanity, and death.

If a pregnant woman has syphilis she can give it to her unborn baby, causing it to be sick, to be deformed, or to die.

Gonorrhea left untreated can cause general bad health, sterility, arthritis, and heart trouble.

Herpes genitalis has been linked to cervical cancer, and can kill newborns.

Be aware of the first signs, such as a sore on the penis or on (or in) the vagina for syphilis and herpes; a discharge (drip) and burning sensation when urinating for gonorrhea. Remember, most women show no signs during the early stages of infection. In both sexes early signs will disappear without treatment after a while. This does not mean you have been cured. If fact, you are getting worse and other symptoms will appear later.

The condom (rubber) when used right is good protection.

Urinating and washing the genitals with soap and hot water right after sex may help.

Syphilis and gonorrhea can be cured. Cure is effective if a doctor starts treatment soon after infection. At the present time there is no cure for herpes, but antibiotic creams and ointments prescribed by a physician will prevent secondary infections and help reduce pain.

Treatment and tracing of VD victims is confidential.

Almost all states have laws that allow teen-agers to be treated without parental consent or knowledge.

Protect Your Lover, Wear a Rubber

18. *What's Fashionable These Days*
It is fashionable these days for unknown or long-forgotten professionals to attribute major evils of our times to the "excesses" of the women's liberation movement. Typical of what is being attributed is:

The human race is committing sexual suicide.

Motherhood rooted in biology and history (or eternity) is being prostituted by women who expect men to share in household and parenting responsibilities, especially when preschool-age children are involved.

We professionals (understood to mean

almost all professionals in a particular field) are treating an *alarmingly* large number of men who are impotent as a result of their relationship with aggressive women.

Bisexuality is only a *cover* for innate or latent homosexuality.

Children are growing up confused to the point of needing psychiatric treatment because they are not sure of their roles in life. This is especially true of girls who want to join the Little League.

The increase in the number of women who commit criminal acts is due to "their" wanting to be more like men.

It's possible to come up with findings such as these by:

1. Reporting on your small sample to a cheap journalist.

2. Creating the impression in the media that we are in imminent danger because everybody is doing it ("it" being, for example, experimenting with bisexuality, women forcing men to change diapers and thus reversing a historic role).

3. Creating nonexistent polarities. If you are not heterosexual, then you must be homosexual.

4. Setting up straw (wo)men by citing isolated incidents or extreme examples or excesses as being typical of the women's movement.

My view is that for every impotent man, suicidal woman, confused child, we now have (as a result of the influence of the women's liberation movement) thousands of liberated people who are finding themselves in a life that they can celebrate.*

Instead of observing trends, some people, as a consequence of their own personal insecurities and limited experience, try to create them.

* Where did I get my statistics? I made them up. They make up theirs and I'll make up mine.

A SEX SUMMARY IN
THE FORM OF EIGHTEEN
SLOGANS AND IDEAS

1. Sex is one of life's celebrations.

2. Mature sex is voluntary, consensual, and enjoyable. Immature sex is involuntary, exploitative, and generally unsatisfying.

3. Everybody develops sexual preferences, for reasons that are not always understood. Everyone is entitled to his or her preferences. Being fearful of any form of sexual behavior is the problem—not the interest or desire for it. Nobody is entitled to exploit another person in order to satisfy his or her own impulses.

4. As a compulsion, sex is at best a drag. As an expression of love, or at least the possibility of love, it is one of life's more pleasurable times —however brief. All really pleasurable experiences are of relatively brief duration, and fortunately they are repeatable.

5. It is possible to have sex without being intimate. Some people use sex as their way of avoiding intimacy. It is also possible to become intimate without having sexual intercourse.

6. There is somebody for everybody. Self-acceptance is the key to being attractive to someone.

7. Sexual intercourse is not all there is to sexuality, nor is the ultimate orgasm, no matter how multiple or simultaneous. Some people achieve their best orgasm by masturbating. The best expression of sexuality is probably when it is shared with another person in terms of how you feel for each other, much more than what you do to each other.

8. Nothing in sexuality is fixed. Sex doesn't have to be impulsive or a disease or an impending disaster. It's even okay to make mistakes.

9. Masturbation is a normal expression of sexuality—no matter how frequently it is done or at what age. It becomes a problem only as a result of guilt. Once is too much if you do not like it.

10. You cannot tell the size of a penis by observing it in a nonerect state. Some hang long; others seem tiny. Some of those that appear quite small erect to larger sizes than those that appear huge while flaccid.

11. Breast size or shape has nothing to do with sexual or personal adequacy.

12. All dreams and impulses are normal. Behavior can be abnormal or immoral, but not thoughts.

13. Guilt is the energy for the obsessive preoccupation with thoughts or the

compulsive preoccupation with behavior you don't enjoy.

14. We are all latent bi-, auto-, hetero-, and homosexuals. Select a sexual life-style that is right for you. Don't settle for "less" because of fears.

15. A homosexual is an adult who has and prefers sexual relations with someone of the same sex. It's not OK to be antigay.

16. Knowledge contributes to responsible sexual behavior; ignorance stimulates the opposite.

17. It would be best if parents were the primary sex educators of their own children. They would be if they became askable. By responding to all questions without being concerned about telling a child too much, parents become askable.

18. Censorship is often a mask to prevent or make illegal something that is controversial, "contrary to parental rights," or "against the laws of nature or God." In turn, these become the stepping-stones for repression of all civil rights. The struggle for a sexually mature society is in its ultimate sense a struggle for freedom of speech and the capacity to live with people who have many different points of view and values.

A BASIC PAPERBACK
SEX EDUCATION LIBRARY*

Barbach, Lonnie Garfield. *For Yourself—The Fulfillment of Female Sexuality.*

Boston Women's Health Book Collective. *Our Bodies, Ourselves.*

Bullough, Vern and Bullough, Bonnie. *Sin, Sickness and Sanity.*

Buscaglia, Leo. *Love.*

Chiappa, J. and Forish, J. *The VD Book.*

Dinnerstein, Dorothy. *The Mermaid and the Minotaur —Sexual Arrangements and Human Arrangements.*

Gagnon, John. *Human Sexualities.*

Goergen, Donald. *The Sexual Celibate.*

Goldberg, Herb. *The Hazards of Being Male.*

Gordon, L. *Woman's Body and Woman's Right.*

Gordon, Sol. *Facts About Sex for Today's Youth.*

Gordon, Sol. *YOU—A Survival Guide for Youth.*

Gordon, Sol. *You Would if You Loved Me.*

Gordon, Sol, and Dickman, Irving R. *Sex Education: The Parent's Role.* (Public Affairs Pamphlet #549)

Gordon, Sol and Libby, Roger W. *Sexuality Today and Tomorrow.*

Gordon, Sol, Scales, Peter, and Everly, Kathleen. *The Sexual Adolescent.*

Hamilton, Eleanor. *Sex with Love: A Guide for Young People.*

* Recommended by The Institute for Family Research and Education, 760 Ostrom Avenue, Syracuse, New York 13210.

Kelly, Gary F. *Learning About Sex—The Contemporary Guide for Young Adults.*

Kennedy, Eugene. *The Heart of Loving.*

Kennedy, Eugene. *The New Sexuality.*

Landers, Ann. *High School Sex and How to Deal with It—A Guide for Teens and Parents.* (Pamphlet)

Mayerhoff, Milton. *On Caring.*

McNeill, John H., S.J. *The Church and the Homosexual.*

Pomeroy, W. B. *Your Child and Sex: A Guide for Parents.*

Sherman, Allan. *The Rape of the APE.*

Tripp, C. A. *The Homosexual Matrix.*

Zilbergeld, Bernie. *Male Sexuality.*

MARRIAGE
SECTION

*You only grow by coming
to the end of something and by
beginning something else.*
—Garp

TEN QUALITIES OF A
SUCCESSFUL MARRIAGE

Tomorrow's family promises to reflect the lessons we have learned in the past. People will marry because they love each other. They will not allow the desire for money or prestige to push them into ill-considered alliances. They will not marry to legitimize unplanned pregnancies. They will not subordinate their own feelings and preferences in a futile quest for parental approval. Without all that excess baggage, without the guilt, fear, and uncertainty that haunt so many relationships today, tomorrow's partners in marriage will be starting out with a definite advantage.

In many key respects, husbands and wives will be equals. The majority will have had comparable education. Most will work outside the home for the greater portion of their adult lives. Of those who consciously decide to have children, most will stop at two and will share the responsibilities of infant and child care.

Before turning specifically to the qualities that characterize dynamic and exciting marriages, I offer, first, a few ground rules in no particular order.

1. The quality of marriage is not in any major way affected by a couple's decision about children. The important thing is for two people to develop their relationship with each other *before* children are born or even contemplated, and to

reaffirm that relationship often through the years no matter what has been decided about children. Thus, my list will make no references to children.

2. There is no end to new beginnings. Even the most tiresome marriage can be restored. To be sure, the passage of time alone does little except to make us older. But it's amazing how time *and* effort *and* a genuine mutual desire for change can bring new happiness and interest into a relationship.

3. One "sure" test of marital happiness is your energy level. Good marriages are energizing. There is time for everything, or almost everything. Happily married people do not scurry about all day long in a hyperactive frenzy, but they do have the will and the energy to be creative and productive. Bad marriages, immature relationships are exhausting for both partners. It seems there is barely time to get a meal on the table. Yet, for all that sense of having raced through the day, it is hard at the end to remember where the hours went.

4. For all the screeching about so-called liberation, the fact is that liberation in its truest sense becomes and enhances those who embrace it. What best distinguishes liberated adults of both sexes from their unliberated neighbors is their freedom to behave, and to behave *well,* to be interesting and interested, to be alternately warm and businesslike, dependent and daring, needed and in need. Liberated men and women have

dignity. They do not feel inferior to others. They will not let themselves be made to feel inferior. At the same time, they are delighted to praise and enjoy the real achievements of other people.

5. Marriage without passion is admittedly dull, but without friendship it is devastating.

6. Conspicuous by their absence from my list are such familiar platitudes as fidelity, exclusivity, total honesty, owning, belonging, total sharing, and "meant for each other."

7. I believe in love, but not when it becomes a burden; in priority, not exclusivity; in sharing, not soul-baring; in deeds, not promises. There has to be space within the marriage commitment. Without it, self-indulgence and exploitation will take root and grow.

Fair enough, you say, but what do all these words look like in real life?

The Big Ten (in order of importance)

1. Love—caring, intimacy, loyalty, and trust during good times and bad, holding strong in the face of illness or stress. It includes such simple things as remembering birthdays, anniversaries, and ordinary courtesies. It means offering to help without being asked. It means saying, "I love you."

2. Learning how and when to laugh—having a sense of humor and keeping it tuned. You had one when you were little. Where did it go? Learn how to laugh again. Practice. Find something funny in a situation that doesn't look funny at all.

3. Making interesting conversation—being sensitive to the interests of your partner, sparing him the office gossip, sparing her the traffic situation on Interstate 80. The key here is the willingness to communicate. Don't be afraid to hurt your partner's feelings or to reveal your own. Express your opinions. If your partner doesn't share them, nothing is lost. If he explains why, so much the better.

4. Together, a passionate sense of mission or purpose about something—an involvement with other people's lives as a means of enhancing your own. It can be anything: a cause, your religion, the environment, politics.

5. Friends together and separately—sharing time and talk with people you both enjoy, being sensitive to the negative chemistry between your partner and some of your closest friends. Learn to cherish some space, privacy, interests, hobbies, and even an occasional vacation of your own.

6. A promise—you will not compromise the person you want to be. You yourself are not negotiable. If you want to have children and stay home with them while they're small, if you'd rather work away from home, or if you want to balance work and family, *do it* and with no apologies. If someone else disapproves and

122

accuses you of wasting your time, it's not your problem unless you agree. If you make it a point not to compromise yourself, it might not be a bad idea to stop trying to analyze the reasons for everything you do. If you know you are happy, why look for reasons to reconsider?

7. Tolerance—for occasional craziness, irritableness, tiredness, clumsiness, memory lapses, human error, disagreement, argument, and very contrary points of view.

8. Willingness to accept each other's style— active in some respects and passive in others. Don't be bound by fixed or predetermined notions X is always a female prerogative or Y always a male imperative.

A man can change diapers, tend sick puppies, respond with pleasure to a woman's sexual initiatives. A woman can change a tire, bring home the bigger paycheck, get the first (or only) Ph.D. in the house. Everyone is entitled to have important friendships with members of either sex without incurring strange glances.

9. Sexual fulfillment—not measured in terms of orgasmic frequency or quality, but as an abiding expression of shared intimacy. It is possible for people who hate each other to have good mechanical sex. And there are deeply devoted couples whose sex lives leave much to be desired. While the sex machines may never learn to like each other, the caring partners can learn to overcome their sexual difficulties—by relaxing and forgoing intercourse for a while in favor of

simple touching, truthful talk about what gives pleasure, a shower for two, listening to music.

Sex is the most grossly overstated "privilege" of marriage. Even today we still hear righteous warnings that sex before marriage leaves nothing to look forward to in marriage. To those who perceive sex as the main benefit of marriage, I'd advise staying single. Getting married isn't worth it.

10. Sharing household tasks—I clean, you cook; I fold, you iron; I mow, you rake. Next week reverse it, or not, as it suits you both.

So, there it is unadorned. Has anything major been left out? Is the order right? Let me know what you think.

I remember one irate man who, on hearing this list, could not believe that sexual fulfillment placed so near the bottom. I replied that of the 5,324 important aspects of marriage, sex was still in the top 10!

Of course, very few marriages are in an optimal state all or even most of the time. Ebbs and flows, ups and downs are part of the human condition. But the partners in good marriages find happiness in striving toward it. This isn't Pollyanna-style gaiety, all sweetness and light with never a blessed break, but a sensible optimism, buoyant and energetic, for at least a part of every day. After all, most of life's peak experiences are of brief duration—a certain look in someone's eyes, a sunset, a newborn's first cry. The rest of the time most of us are just too busy living.

In the final analysis, marriage might best be seen as a journey in which two people together, and at times separately, discover what life has to offer. There is a growing sense that the past is past and that life is not a meaning but an opportunity for meaningful experiences. While traditions, rituals, observances, and flexible roles can give marriage structure and purpose, they can never substitute for loving, caring, kindness, loyalty, and having fun together.

PLAYING
WITH WORDS
AND IDEAS
SECTION

If you have nothing to do,
don't do it here.

I play with words
and ideas. Do you?

If you need a pickup,
Pick up someone.

Not everything
I remember
happened.

Maybe it happened
the way you said it did
But that's not the way
it affected me.

Why me?
Because
it's you we're
after.

Nothing works anymore.
Of course not—
Poor workmanship.

Criminals should serve
society,
not time.

FOUR UNIMPORTANT
BUT DELECTABLE FANTASIES

If I could reign supreme,
in order of unimportance

1. I would remove all the fig leaves
from the Vatican art museum
in Rome and make all the
people responsible
for those aesthetic atrocities
eat them.

2. For people who wear their smiles
on their buttons instead of
their faces,
    I would wipe their smiles
off their buttons.

3. People who finish their sentences
with *whatever* would be assigned

1,000 times to write the sentence—
"I will never use the word *whatever* for
any reasons whatsoever, ever, ever, again."

4. I would cause all rude
clerks, wait(ers) (resses),
attendants, sales personnel,
bureaucrats, supervisors,
and administrators to be
behaviorally modified by
getting a rather severe
electric shock in their
asses each time they are
unresponsive to the public
they are supposed to serve.

TRAVEL VARIATIONS
ON THE SAME THEME

I

The countryside is
     tranquil
     only if the mind is.

II

When the mind is troubled
the tranquillity of nature
becomes a storm,
but sometimes
I forget
what's on my mind
to allow nature to
emerge
serene.

SOBER THOUGHTS ON
JULY FOURTHS

First

If someone means well,
Even if you can't praise it,
    affirm it.
    Be it
a television program,
a column in the newspaper,
a helpful direction,
a smile.

Second

On the other hand.

Third

Life is full of contradictions.
The more you try to reconcile them,
the less successful
you will be. Leave it be.

Fourth

Well done is better than
    well said.
        —*Ben Franklin*

And so Fourth

It's better to be
    pissed off
than pissed on.

Back 'n' Fourth

Some things are better left unsaid.
Some things are better left undone.

DIAGNOSIS

I don't think the present psychiatric diagnostic system fits most people who are labeled by it. I have, therefore, in response to popular demand created my own.

If for some reason or other a person can't be described as normal then one of these four categories will most assuredly fit:

tight-assed,
smart-ass,
boring,
mean.

SPIRITUAL
SECTION

---

*People who think they
have found the meaning of
life are usually people who
are just plain mean.*

THERE IS A
WAY FOR EVERYONE

People who want to
mock God
    say there is only
    one road to Him.

Lord knows, for Him
    a one-way sign is a
    dead end
    leading to nowhere.

Lord knows,
    there are infinite ways to find
    your own way.

IS YOUR RELIGION ORGANIZED?

Being religious isn't worth much
if God doesn't help you
become a friend
to at least one other person
and a member of a society
that cares about people.

VARIETIES OF
RELIGIOUS EXPERIENCES

Prayer for the dead

Whenever I think about dead people I care about,
they get points up there.

It's an irrational idea,
but somehow I'm comforted
by the thoughts of my unhappy parents
scoring in the celestial heavens.

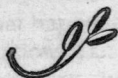

FORTUNATELY NOT EVERY
DAY IS IMPORTANT

Alone

> feeling sorry for
> the plants
> unwatered
> like my love
> in the Fall of
> life

I

> seek the sun
> among withered flowers
> and brief encounters
> where friendship lingers
> not for long.
> I am loved
> not enough to still the
> Exile. I lit two candles to

Find

> The way. No one noticed.
> What is a way to a
> Jewish holiday?
> Then

God

> responded, somewhat impatiently
> I thought,
> "For Heavens Sake, Water The
> Plants, And Get On With It."

Erev Hanukkah 1978

GOD WON'T STAND FOR IT

What's the point of finding God
If you can't find anyone else?

You can't use God to
validate who you are.
(God won't stand for it.)

AUTOBIOGRAPHICAL SECTION

If someone asks me, "Can I trust you?"
I say, "No."

I FEEL SORRY FOR PEOPLE

Who
     can't say thank you,
     can't accept anyone
being nice to them;

     Who don't understand
that sometimes
     telling the truth
is an expression of
hostility;

     Who don't know
that much of what is called relevance
is boring;

     Who can't stand
being alone sometimes;

     Who are impulse-
ridden;

     Who are relentlessly preoccupied with the
motives
of others;

     Who have
experienced love only
as a burden.

homage to rita

my friend rita
lives
at the chelsea,
as did
sarah bernhardt,
mark twain,
o. henry,
edgar lee masters,
brendan behan,
dylan thomas,
arthur miller,
thomas wolfe,
virgil thompson.

my friend rita,
often troubled,
calls me
long distance;
short intimate talks
make her
feel better,
me worse.

that's rita
at the chelsea,

sick,
unhappy,
but
living
a fuller,
exciting life,
with love affairs, fire alarms, and
more people who adore her
than anyone I know.

rita at the chelsea
knows how to live it up
but not down.
but that's rita,
my friend,
the artist
among artists
at the chelsea.

WILL YOU BE MY FRIEND?

A friend gave me
a gift—
James Kavenaugh's
poem book,
"Will you be
my friend?"

I didn't go for it much.

Another friend gave
me a gift—
James Kavenaugh's
poem book
"Will you be my friend?"

I said yes
and liked the book a lot,
especially the
"Solemn Psychologist."

The people I like the best come in all sizes, shapes,
and sexes, but all are

devoted to a good cause* and/or have a passionate
        interest in at least one thing,
mainly optimistic,
generous with their time,
receptive to humor,
easily communicative,
able to risk brief encounters,
enthusiastic about something important in their
        lives,
interested in me.

* As I would define it.

FRAGMENTS

Some people genuinely like being helpful.
They get pleasure out of helping, giving, teaching.
They are so pleased if you are pleased when they
     go out of their way for you.
My wife's like that.
She is a really good person who is pleased when
     I'm pleased with the good things she's done
     for me—rather unselfishly, it appears to me.

I'm different. Mind you, I help people too—
     Perhaps more than she does.
But my motives are not always so unselfish (mind
     you, I said not always; that doesn't mean
     never).
That's why some people get angry with me after
     a while, especially when I do a wrong thing.
Now, you'd think they'd remember all the good
     things I did for them and let me get away
     with this wrong thing.
But no, they get very angry and take advantage of
     me and try to hurt me (I am vulnerable).
This sort of thing almost never happens to my
     wife.

That's one of the reasons why I avoid intimacy
 with most of the people who want to become
 intimate with me.
That's one of the reasons a few people reject
 intimacy with me because they sense that I'm
 not good for them.
And yet you wouldn't guess it from first
 impressions of me.

LINES MY
MOTHER TAUGHT ME

Eat.

Is today tomorrow?

So far so good.

Cheap is expensive.

How do you know?

As you make your bed, so shall you sleep in it.

(And, in desperation:) Go bang your head against
the wall.

AND LINES MY
FATHER TAUGHT ME

Don't upset your mother.

It could be this, it could be that.

Don't worry, it'll all turn out for the best.

(Or, in desperation:) The trouble with you is
you've had it too good.

IN MY LIFE THERE
IS ROOM (IN A WORD) FOR

joy
moods
repression
guilt
vibrations
love
God
peaks
anger
music
friends
laziness
malingering
grief
laughter
sharing
selfishness
conversations
privacy
eating
aloneness
compassion
conviviality
culture
teaching
learning
fear
sleeping
stupidity

mistakes
wisdom
insights
sex
boasting
worry
memories
poetry
assertiveness
reading
exercise
introspection
leisure
illness
order
ritual
nostalgia
study
contemplation
hobbies
tranquillity
creativity
individuality
discipline
pride
fantasy
expediency
depression
family

touching
nature
pets
charity
warmth
intimacy
politeness
dreaming
fun
vitality
enthusiasm
hope
luck
optimism
excitement
caring
mystery
immaturity
defenses
work
wisdom
reconciliation
awe
admiration
forgiveness
pain
prayer
achievement
remorse

challenge	sadness	aggravation
regrets	celebration	interference
stimulation	dignity	kindliness
agony	effervescence	repetition
deprivation	forgetfulness	sociability
ignorance	conflict	humility
naivety	humor	change
relaxation	goodness	

And in Your Own Life—

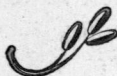

I TRY TO AVOID
(BUT NOT ALWAYS SUCCESSFULLY)

hate

jealousy

envy

exploitation

hurting

procrastination

accidents

gossip

aggressiveness

forgetting

pretentiousness

loneliness

prejudice

belligerence

hostility

lawlessness

contemptuousness

boredom

anxiety

despair

greed

drugs

coldness

impoliteness

callousness

insensitivity

arrogance

hypocrisy

pity

banality

apathy

uncaring

gloating

complaining

Now, make your own list—

Really believe the stories they make up about the
    "good old days."
Have the answer.
Are born again (without a new vision).
Have found IT.
Boast a lot.
Talk too much.
Say they are busy.
Are greedy.
Have nothing to do.
Make a virtue of not being well informed.
Are sanctimonious.
Are pompous, self-righteous, smart-assed
    columnists like Evans and Novak, Andrew
    Greeley, and Michael Novak.
Pretend they are fair and really not reactionary
    (I much prefer William Buckley, who is
    pompous, self-righteous, and admits it).
Quote the Bible (selectively) to justify their own
    narrow minds.
Are jealous
    or envious
    or live a life of regrets.
Gossip.
Think this country is going to the dogs
    or that it belongs to them.
Pose as rites to life or john birch trees.
Are contemptuous of me because of my popularity
    or notoriety, as the case may be.

Question: Why, On the Day of Atonement,
is the confession of sins given
in alphabetical order?
Answer: If it were otherwise we should
not know when to stop beating our
breast. For there is no end to sin,
and no end to the awareness of sin,
but there *is* an end to the alphabet.
—*A Hasidic saying*

A quiet day of fasting and meditation inspires noble thoughts.

Of course, it is easy to be a noble thoughts hero and hard to be an everyday human being.

At the synagogue the Rabbi spoke about Abraham. God commanded Abraham to sacrifice his son, Isaac, and Abraham agreed. "Was this evil?" asked the Rabbi. Of course it was, but to disobey the Lord seemed to Abraham a greater evil, perhaps even an unthinkable evil.

In the midst of my noble thoughts an unthinkable thought came to me.

Are not most of our important decisions based on a choice between evils? I decide not to give my wealth to the poor. I share with my own sense of time and little sacrifice on my part. In the meantime, people are hungry and some die. Of course, I think I give more to charity than anyone else I know. But that's not the point!

What is the point?

I'm not sure.

THE KIND OF
PEOPLE I DON'T LIKE MUCH

The ones who

know the cost of everything but the value of nothing.

let you know what's wrong with the world, but won't put a bit of energy into changing what's wrong in their own lives, let alone their own neighborhoods.

are so preoccupied with themselves that they have not the slightest interest in what others do, think, or feel.

boast a lot. (I don't like myself when I do it.)

NO REGRETS?

Every once in a while you read in the papers about old-timers reminiscing about life. The thing that gets me is when they say, "I have no regrets."

It sounds so phony to me. Here I am only fifty-five—far from dying or being old—and I have lots of regrets.

Here are my ten most regrettable regrets, in order of regrettableness:

1. Very private. Can't reveal it just yet.
2. Not being as nice as I should have been to my parents.
3. Four or five people I've hurt and I know they'll never forgive me.
4. Not having been deeply immersed in my religion.
5. Not having learned two foreign languages (I should have taken my Hebrew and French lessons seriously).
6. Not having learned to dance.
7. Not having learned to swim.
8. Not having developed an expertise in one subject, like a Renaissance painting, white wines, a philosopher, a period of Jewish history.
9. Giving a job to someone I felt sorry for.
10. Not taking the trouble to go to Washington for the big Peace March.

There are, of course, hundreds of other regrets but I'm too busy with my life now to be preoccupied with them. Those are regrets over which I had some measure of control. There are also regrets over matters I couldn't help or put into effect no matter how hard I tried. For example, I would like by now to be famous (author of best sellers, appear on the "Tonight" show, be able to say hello to Woody Allen, and stuff like that). And I wouldn't mind being independently wealthy so I wouldn't have to work for a living.

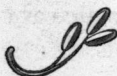

MOVING EXPERIENCES

The experience that affected me more than any other during the last ten years was the July 4, 1976, rescue of the Jews at Entebbe, which moved me to tears.

Here are the runners-up:
Two Plays
> *Equus*
> *For Colored Girls Who Have Considered Suicide When the Rainbow is Enuf* (especially the part, "somebody almost walked off wid alla my stuff")

Two Films
> *Outrageous*
> *The Seven Beauties*

One Talk
> Elie Wiesel on the Holocaust

One Book
> *The Survivors—An Anatomy of Life in the Death Camps* by Terrence des Pres

One Person
> Pierra Vejjabul in Bangkok, Thailand, the heroic godmother of thousands of unwanted and rejected children born to Thai mothers and American fathers who abandoned them

And a glimpse at two autobiographies
> Susan Sontag and Richard Brooks
> Susan Sontag at 45 years of age found that the

crisis of cancer added a fierce intensity to
her life. "Death is part of the dignity and
seriousness of life."
Richard Brooks—bemoaning the fact that he
didn't have much to do with his parents
when they were alive: "All my tears for
them are bullshit; they mean nothing.
Maybe I can help somebody else, take care
of somebody else, think of somebody else,
love somebody else while they're *alive*—
right now, a little less hating, a little more
caring. Why can't we ever learn it? We hide
from it all the time."

From an interview in the
Advocate, *January 11, 1978*

My inner moving experiences are still private and
have to do with personal grief, personal
exhilaration, of moments totally without
inhibitions in a strange country,
personal joy and affirmation of my love for Judith,
and the brief but still rewarding excitement of a
reconnection with two formerly intimate friends.

At another level,
I've been impressed with and thrilled by
hundreds of experiences—not the least of which
was reading *To Have or To Be* by Erich
Fromm, and Eugene Kennedy's *The Heart of
Loving,*
Ragtime by E. L. Doctorow,

and *The World According to Garp* by John
   Irving,
and was surprised by the discovery of
The Mason Williams Reading Matter.
   I loved his one-liner:
   "Soon you begin to realize that 'I don't want
to' is the world's greatest reason."
   Another very exciting book was *How to Save
Your Own Life* by Erica Jong. I loved her list:

1. Renounce useless guilt.
2. Don't make a cult of suffering.
3. Live in the now (or at least in the soon).
4. Always do the things you fear the most.
   Courage is an acquired taste like caviar.
5. Trust all joy.
6. If the evil eye fixes you in its gaze, look
   elsewhere.
7. Get ready to be eighty-seven.
           (to be continued)

I enjoyed *Saturday Night Fever* with John Travolta.
   (His life story fills me with awe.)

And just for my own pleasure let me recall
      sights of the last few years (and let the people
I was with note that I have not forgotten)
      the Danish countryside near Eskebjerg,
      wandering the old city of Copenhagen and
         then Stockholm,
      Varmland in Sweden,

London and Cotswold country (Cirencester
   and Burford), marvelous Cambridge and
   Ely,
Kyoto and Wakura Spa,
Singapore briefly,
Penang more so,
Hanging Rock in Australia,
Melbourne and Sydney,
New Zealand for other reasons,
Bangkok the best.
Los Angeles is special,
Long Beach is special,
Jerusalem is holy,
Rome says it,
but New York City more so for me.

Dear Lord,

I've made mistakes.

I've trusted people who took advantage of me.
I've helped people who didn't appreciate me.
I've done good things for people who are now
    contemptuous of me.
I've gone out of my way for people who wouldn't
    lift a finger for me.
I've hurt people without intending to do so. And
    they have taken revenge.
I've wounded people whom I have loved but not
    well enough, and the wounds have not
    healed.
I've loved people who have responded with hate.

I'm sorry for all the people I have hurt. I feel sorry
    for all the people who have hurt me.
What was, was.
It couldn't have been otherwise.
I'm human. I make mistakes.
Forgive me, dear Lord,
Even if I know what I do.
I'll try to do better the next time.
But I can't promise
I'll be good
All the time.

Life goes on.

MY LAST WILL AND TESTAMENT

If I die
before I'm ready
I ask
forgiveness
of those I've hurt
without having
made amends.
If I'm not ready
it doesn't matter
that much.
There is no one who
can't get along without me.
If there are regrets
neither you nor I
can do anything more.
But this I do request.
If I die
before my heart or brain
documents it
let me be without
extraordinary means.
Don't keep my useless body
technically alive.
Only relieve the pain

and let me die.
Don't want no busybody
busy with my body.
Tak
for Alt.*

June 12, 1978

* Danish "Thanks for Everything." It commonly appears on
tombstones in Denmark.

POLITICAL
SECTION

(EDITORIALIZING
ON SUNDRY SUBJECTS)

What you do affects everyone.

THE HOLOCAUST

The most horrendous single example in human
history of mass murder was the *Holocaust*—the
calculated extermination of six million European
Jews by the Nazis. No barbarism of ancient times,
no blood lust of "primitive" peoples, no bizarre
atrocities unearthed by anthropologists has ever
approached the inhuman evils committed by the
Nazis and their allies—all representatives of
"highly civilized" European cultures.

Is there any purpose in dwelling on this
terrible chapter in human history, in constantly
reviving painful memories of the past? Students of
history and of human behavior believe that there
is. Terrence des Pres in his eloquent book, *The
Survivors*, attempts to "bear witness" and to offer
some sense of what happened. In one moving
passage, he writes:

> Death is compounded by oblivion, and the
> foundation of humanness—faith in human
> continuity—is endangered. The final horror is that
> no one will be left. A survivor of Dachau told me
> this:
>
>> The SS guards took pleasure in telling us that we
>> had no chance of coming out alive, a point they

emphasized with particular relish by insisting that after the war the rest of the world would not believe what happened; there would be rumors, speculations, but no clear evidence, and people would conclude that evil on such a scale was just not possible.

Without the past we have nothing to stand on, no context from which to organize the energies of moral vision. Against such possibilities survivors do what they can. Facing man-made horror, their need becomes strong to remember and record—to ensure, through their own survival or the survival of their word, that out of horror's very midst (from where else can it come?) the truth shall emerge.

Elie Wiesel, himself a survivor of the Holocaust, has written many books to "bear witness" to the truth. In *Beggar in Jerusalem* the hero crawls out of a mass grave and makes his way to Israel, where he becomes a connection between the past and the present. The message of Wiesel is that if we forget, it can happen again. There are no explanations, Wiesel says, only stories, legends—and memories.

MY COMMENTARIES ON FOUR
IMPORTANT DOCUMENTS DEALING
WITH HUMAN RIGHTS

I
UN Declaration of the Rights of the Child
(International Year of the Child 1979)

The Right
> to affection, love, and understanding.
> to adequate nutrition and medical care.
> to free education.
> to full opportunity for play and recreation.
> to a name and nationality.
> to special care, if handicapped.
> to be among the first to receive relief in times of disaster.
> to learn to be a useful member of society and to develop individual abilities.
> to be brought up in a spirit of peace and universal brotherhood.
> to enjoy these rights, regardless of race, color, sex, religion, national or social origin.

I would add the right of a woman not to give birth to a child who is unwanted, who is certainly expected to be born severely deformed or retarded, who is the product of rape, whose birth would endanger the life of the mother, or whose chances of survival due to poverty or neglect are minimal.

United States Supreme Court   January 22, 1973

"We recognize the right of the individual, married or single, to be free from unwarranted governmental intrusion into matters so fundamentally affecting a person as the decision whether to bear or beget a child. That right necessarily includes the right of a woman to decide whether or not to terminate her pregnancy."

Abortion is a religious, moral, and constitutional issue. People do not, and cannot be expected to, agree on a single position or attitude toward it. But since separation of church and state is an integral part of our democracy, and since democracy thrives amid difference, I am very angry at those elements in our society that are trying to impose their views on everyone else. Such people threaten the very essence of a democratic society that is based on freedom of choice whenever possible.

III
Proposed Equal Rights Amendment

"Equality of rights under law shall not be denied or abridged by the United States or any state on account of sex."

The tremendous roadblocks put up to prevent passage of this amendment are a tragic commentary on our residual antifeminist attitudes.

IV
Resolution on Library Services for Youth

Passed by the American Library Association Council, Midwinter Meeting, 1978

"Whereas services to youth are recognized as a basic component of professional librarianship; and

Whereas library censorship problems consistently occur in connection with sex-related information for youth; and

Whereas it has been documented that the onset of puberty is occurring approximately four months earlier each decade; and

Whereas this early maturation has led to earlier sexual exploration and pressure among children and adolescents, with especially severe consequences for girls; and

Whereas adolescent pregnancy has reached epidemic proportions so as to be recognized as a target area of concern by the U.S. Public Health Service; and

Whereas social responsibility and support of intellectual freedom are acknowledged to be priorities of the ALA:

Therefore, be it RESOLVED THAT:

ALA hereby affirms the right of youth to comprehensive, sex-related education, materials, programs, referral and health services of the highest quality; and

ALA hereby affirms the active role of

librarians in providing sex-related education, materials, programs and referral services; and

ALA urges librarians and library educators to reexamine existing policies and practices, and to assume a leadership role in seeing that information is available for children and adolescents, their parents, and youth-serving professionals at the state and local level, to assure that comprehensive sex-related education materials, programs, referral and health services for youth are available and publicized; and

ALA offer this resolution to the Planned Parenthood Federation of America Inc. for inclusion in their POSITIVE POLICY HANDBOOK of organization statements supporting sexual health and education services for youth."

We have to be alert to bigots and book-burners who are trying to decide for the rest of us what is appropriate to read. We need to spread the rumor that the First Amendment still lives.

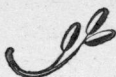

If you want to take a
stand about Israel,
give three facts plus one question some thought:

1. Almost every adult living in Israel now is a *survivor* either of the Holocaust or
of a flight from Moslem countries
and/or has lost a son or a father in one of four
recent wars.

2. The Western democracies made very little
effort to save Jews during World War II and even
turned back to the gas chambers boatloads of Jews
who escaped.

3. The Western democracies kept none of
their promises related to the establishment of a
Jewish homeland—did nothing when five Arab
nations violated the United Nations Declaration in
1953.

Question: Why is it that only Israel is
expected to give up everything it WINS in wars it
didn't start or want?

ABOUT DEATH

The basic theme of this book is how to cope more effectively with the problems of living. In order to do so, however, it seems appropriate to say something about death.

Death is very much "in" these days. It is discussed far more openly than in earlier generations, and from many points of view. Much emphasis is given to the "right to die with dignity" when life no longer seems to hold any meaning, as in cases of terminal illness. Some philosophers have even suggested that one must come to terms with the inevitability of death before life can be fully appreciated.

For me, however, the opposite holds true. The existential question is not death but *life*. Only people who fully appreciate life can understand death. Nor is it necessary to accept death "gracefully"—only its inevitability.

We are deeply affected when someone close to us dies. The grief and the mourning are not futile. They are part of caring for ourselves and sharpen our own respect for life.

From a psychological point of view, the most important fact to understand about the death of someone for whom you care deeply is this: Your first impulse, in all probability, will be *to feel guilty about it*.

It's all right to have regrets that perhaps you didn't do enough for the deceased or didn't show enough love, respect, or kindness. But you shouldn't allow such feelings to hang you up for too long. Look at it this way: If you feel bad because your relationship with this person wasn't all that you would have liked, the only sensible thing to do now is to *improve your relationships with the living people around you.*

Many people carry a burden of *irrational* guilt after the death of a loved one. For example, a young woman who was away at college when her mother died may become obsessed with the idea that perhaps things would have turned out differently if only she had remained home. Such an impulse to feel guilty, however illogical, is understandable. The important thing is not to freeze on it.

Deaths of older people are in a sense expected and to some are relatively easy to take. But many deaths come unexpectedly and prematurely. The emotional distress this causes is part of living. When the immediate shock has passed, *your obligation is still to the living.*

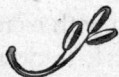

ON BEING HANDICAPPED

If you are not yourself "handicapped" in some way, you very probably know someone, a relative or friend, who is. According to the "American Coalition of Citizens with Disabilities," about 36 million Americans today—roughly one in six—suffer serious physical, mental, or emotional impairment.

Being handicapped is not easy. It involves all kinds of difficulties—social, emotional, sexual, and, of course, economic. Part of the problem is that *handicapped people are often excluded from the mainstream of life by the rest of us.*

As a psychologist who has worked for more than a quarter of a century with the problems of handicapped people, I have some advice. First, to people who are not disabled: Make an effort to befriend a handicapped person. Do this not from pity but with empathy and compassion, as an aspect of being a decent human being. Form your friendship on the basis of a common interest, or by helping the person to develop an interest in something you already enjoy. Once a real relationship has been established, don't treat the handicapped person with exaggerated delicacy or sensitivity. This is likely to do more harm than good. In particular, don't hesitate to convey frankly what pleases and displeases you. For example, you may find that your new friend is "overdoing it," or misinterpreting your friendly interest for love. If this is so, the sooner and more decisively you straighten things out, the better.

Here is another important point: It's all right to start out feeling uncomfortable. Very few people can be fully comfortable at first in the company of someone who is blind, deaf, or cerebral-palsied. By acknowledging your discomfort, you can bypass pity, shame, guilt, rejection, or withdrawal. Talk about your discomfort, and then your friend may be able to explain, directly or indirectly, how to deal with it.

Now a few "messages" to a person who is handicapped:

1. No one can make you feel inferior without your consent.

2. If you have interests, someone will be interested in you.

3. If you are chronically bored, you will be boring to be with.

4. If you have nothing to do, don't do it with anyone else around.

5 (and most important). Our society does not give you "points" for being handicapped. You need to work hard to make friends and to prove to everybody—

that you are a person first.

that your handicap is secondary to everything that is important to you.

TOWARD A MORATORIUM
ON INTERPRETATION

It is said that teen-age girls
have babies because
of unresolved oedipal complexes.
    I say a teen-ager gets pregnant
because she has a sexual
intercourse.

It is said that in some cultures
men need to impregnate
women in order to prove
their masculinity.
This is called machismo.
    I would call it rape.

It is said in psychiatric
circles that
many people suffer
from disorders that are
latent. The fashionable
latencies these days

are latent
homosexuality and latent
schizophrenia.
     I say that latency is a
figment of the psychiatric
imagination.
You might as well
say all women are
latently pregnant.
If you have an unconscious fear
of dogs, does that make
you a latent dog?

It is said that a male
who murders young males
is a homosexual murderer.
     I say he is a plain murderer.
Is a male who murders young
females
a heterosexual murderer?

An American patriot once said, "If we don't hang together, we're going to hang separately."

If you scratch the surface of somebody who's antigay, you're going to find an anti-E.R.A., anti-Jew, antiblack, and antichoice. Those who oppose gay rights do so on "moral grounds." They quote the Bible and wave their flags. All of their efforts, they claim, are aimed at protecting "the children."

The scenario is not unique. We saw the combination of the Bible, the flag, and the children used in the purging of Jews. We saw it used in the attempt to stop the teaching of evolution in the schools. We see it today in the fight against women's rights and in the battle to keep sex education out of schools.

In each case the opposition fears *choice*. Wrapped securely in the banner of "God and Country," they claim the population will "go the way of Rome" if we allow people to be gay, allow people to be Jewish, allow women to think for themselves, allow children to learn the basic principles of sexuality.

Our message has to be that it is *immoral* to be antigay, antiblack, anti-Jew, anti-E.R.A., anti-sex education. Our message must be that the Bible and the flag and the children do not belong to the opposition but to those who are working to protect individual rights.

The essence of the Bible is love and justice.

The essence of democracy is the basic rights of *all* persons to life, liberty, and the pursuit of happiness. How are these served by the goal of the opposition to eliminate choice, eliminate civil rights, eliminate knowledge?

The gay rights struggle is one of the most crucial battles being fought today. If we lose it, we lose ground in every other cause we hold to be sacred. And we will lose it unless we begin hanging together.

Anita Bryant quotes the Bible in her campaign against gays. She says that God told her to do it. She also said God told her all non-Christians are going to hell. Her finances come from the same people who finance all right-wing causes. If she weren't being taken so seriously, she would be laughable. But when she is named "Woman of the Year" by the readers of *Good Housekeeping,* she isn't funny anymore.

Gay civil rights ordinances have been overwhelmingly defeated in the United States by voters who don't want gay men and lesbians teaching in public schools and living wherever they wish. Opposition is based upon the fear that gays will be "role models," that they'll molest children, that they'll show up in the classroom in a dress (if they are men), and upon the belief that God *hates* homosexuals.

Allowing the majority to vote on the rights of the minority is a dangerous precedent that threatens each and every one of us, most especially when that majority is so misinformed.

Molestation of children is a heterosexual crime more than 90 percent of the time, and usually involves a father and a young daughter. Wearing the clothing of the opposite gender is called transvestism, and every statistic we have indicates it is mainly a *heterosexual* phenomenon. Do we, then, armed with this information, suggest *heterosexuals* shouldn't be teachers? No. To do so would be absurd. How much more absurd, then, is the fear of homosexuals!

And what is this about role models? Are there no straight role models? If there are 100 teachers and 4 are gay, are we to presume that all of the students will flock to the 4 gay teachers for a role model? I don't understand the logic. Gay people tell us they went through twelve and sixteen years of school with allegedly only straight role models and yet they still came out happy, healthy homosexuals. Are the straight students less secure with their sexuality?

When all else fails, the opposition grabs the Bible and quotes from Genesis, Leviticus, and Paul's letters to Romans, Corinthians, and Timothy. Yet, according to the Committee on Sexuality of the Catholic Theological Society of America and other prominent theologians of all denominations, the supposed antigay statements in the Bible have been frequently mistranslated and taken out of context.

President Carter has stated, "I don't see homosexuality as a threat to the family." To my knowledge, he's the first important person who has said that. Carter says, "What has caused the highly publicized confrontation on homosexuality is the desire of homosexuals for the rest of society to approve and add its acceptance of homosexuality as a normal sexual relationship. I don't feel it's a normal sexual relationship." But then he adds, ". . . but at the same time I don't feel that society, through its laws, ought to abuse or harass the homosexual."

The issue is not that homosexuals desire acceptance of homosexuality as a normal sexual relationship. The main thing gay people are worried about is the question of rights. If some or most people don't think it's normal, I'm not worried about that. I have serious questions about celibates, but celibates are not really worried about my questions. They think they're normal and they may well be.

There is one preferred definition of a homosexual, the way I feel about it, and that is "an adult who has and prefers relations with members of the same sex." Period. I don't know if we need a fancy explanation. But after all of the research that I have been able to review, hormonal and hereditary explanations don't hold. All we know is that homosexuals were probably raised by heterosexual parents.

The issue is political. I am vitally concerned with the politics of this question because I am a sex educator. And I want to tell you something about being a sex educator. We don't get too much in the way of hate mail, but 90 percent of all the hate mail we get is anti-Semitic. Here is a typical letter.

> "Sex education in the schools is a filthy and obscene thing. No stranger has a right to talk about fornication to any child or teenager. To do so is to contribute to the delinquency of a minor. It's just a plot on the part of the Jews to first destroy the gentile family and then this gentile nation. It is succeeding only too well. May a curse be upon all of these sons of bitches.

You know this person is also antigay. He is for compulsory pregnancy. He is antiblack, and that's the message we have to get across to people: that this is a conspiracy of the people who are bigots. We have to caution our old friends in the civil rights movement and say, "When they finish with the gays they're coming after the Jews and then the blacks and then women's rights. Let's stick together; let's not let these bigots deny us the unity that we all need because, if we're not going to stick together, we're going to hang separately."

THINGS
AND
STUFF
SECTION

Cheap is expensive.

Did you ever wonder
why "things" seem to come in sevens or tens?

How would *you* go about finding out what the

      seven deadly sins,
      seven wonders of the ancient world,
      Ten Commandments of the Old
         Testament,
      ten articles of the Bill of Rights of the
         American Constitution

                            are?

AN OPEN LETTER TO
JIMMY CARTER

Dear Mr. President,

I love this country but I don't have to tell you that we are in a lot of trouble—would you please become our leader and lead us in a crusade?

Could we start with the things you spoke about to a Bible class on Sunday, September 30, 1977?

> hard work
> clean streets
> planting of flowers
> cleaning up a neighborhood
> respect for authority
> respect for law
> the value of human compassion

I think if we could get started with flowers, everything else would not seem so improbable.

Please—

With best wishes,
Sol Gordon
January 1, 1979

I asked my college students to record for me the lines that their parents use that represent, at least to some extent, their relationships with them. Here is a representative sample.

Mother	Father
Have you met a Jewish boy?	Be careful.
Life is tough all over.	Stop procrastinating.
Is your room in order?	He's not good enough for you.
I live for my children.	Bills, bills, bills!
Count your blessings.	Moderation, moderation . . .
Shut off the noise box!	For crying out loud!
Go lie down.	Rise and shine.
What has that got to do with the price of eggs?	That's what makes chocolate and vanilla.
Think about what you're doing before you do it.	Life is too short to be miserable.
Quit hitting your sister.	Shit, a cat's ass.
OK.	Boys are like buses; one comes along every fifteen minutes.
Go ask your father.	You have a head like a sieve.
We never did that when we were young.	
A watched pot never boils.	

Mother	Father
God is big—have faith.	You're lucky you weren't alive thirty years ago.
Cut your neck.	Don't shoot the bull.
Wait until your father gets home.	Be your own boss—be successful.
And you ask me why I'm so nervous?	Go kill yourself.
Never a dull moment.	Let's keep it down.
I don't care what anybody else does.	You can't be superman all the time.
Be careful.	God give me strength.
All's well that ends well.	Go ask your mother.
The Lord will make a way.	Have the world by the tail.
	Be quiet.
You get more with honey than you do with vinegar.	I've got to deal with the white man.
I'm not your entertainment committee.	You deserve a skinhead.
	There is only one thing money can't buy—poverty.
Definitely not!	Whatever you do, don't!
What do you expect me to do . . . stand on my head and spit nickles?	Go ask your mother.

196

Mother	Father
Mother	*Father*

You don't know how lucky you are.

Enjoy yourself.

Whose turn to feed the dog?

We are not everybody. We are the (family name).

Most mothers would say "Be good," but if being bad makes you happy, be bad. Just be happy.

The only friend you have is yourself and your family.

I'm crazy about you.

L'chaim.

You've got too much.

You're not using your talents to the utmost.

The few times I'm wrong, I admit it.

When I say "Get in the car," get in the car.

When will I have grandchildren?

Life isn't fair.

Be a nice boy and watch out for your ass.

Work hard and party hearty.

Yucky.

Brat.

You're not using your talents to the utmost.

The young gentlemen aren't working today.

Stand on your head and spit Chiclets.

Are you going to say "Good Morning"?

I'm sick of the kids.

Oh, bother.

Oh, sugar.

I'll smack you along side of your head.

I'm going to crown you kids.

Get that dog out of here.

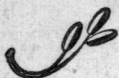

WHAT TO DO
WHEN YOU FIND IT

Mark it.

Make it.

Shake it.

Forsake it.

Hold it.

Fake it.

Bag it.

Take it.

Bury it.

Show it off.

Sock it to 'em.

Don't stand for it.

Sit on it.

Hang onto it.

Cool it.
Toy with it.
Handle it with care.
Play with it.
Sell it.
Love it.
Share it.
Shove it.
Don't knock it.
Drop it.
Damn it.
Do it.
Tell it.

dietdietdietdietdietdietdietdietdietdietdietdietdiet
dietdietdietdietdietdietdietdietdietdietdietdietdiet
dietdietdietdietdietdietdiet

dietdietdietdietdietdietdietdietdietdietdietdietdiet
dietdiet buy it dietdietdietdietdietdietdietdietdiet
dietdietdietdietdietdiet

dietdietdietdietdietdietdietdietdietdietdietdietdiet
dietdietdietdietdietdietdietdiet dye it dietdietdiet
dietdietdietdietdiet

WHAT PEOPLE
ARE DOING WITH IT

Pilots get it up higher.
Divers do it deeper.
Teachers do it with class.
Nurses do it with care.
Drag racers do it faster.
Rowers use longer strokes.
Oysters do it in bed.
Gourmets do it with taste.
Spies do it under cover,
and
Lawyers do it just in case.

Edward de Bono, a philosopher and known as the originator of the concept of lateral thinking, edited a book entitled *The Great Thinkers—The Thinking Minds That Shaped Our Civilization* (G. P. Putnam's Sons, 1976).

Here is his list:

> Moses, Confucius, Plato, Aristotle, Euclid, Jesus, Augustine, Aquinas, Columbus, Machiavelli, Copernicus, Luther, Bacon, Descartes, Newton, Rousseau, Kant, Clerk Maxwell, William James, Nietzsche, Pavlov, Freud, Einstein, Keynes, Norbert Wiener, Sartre, Malthus, Clausewitz, Darwin, Marx

How many of these people are you familiar with—or have you even heard of?

Interesting observation—no women.

Who would you add to this list?

SOME REALLY GOOD
NONFICTION THAT COULD
TURN YOU ON
(to more of the same)

Psychobabble—Fast Talk and Quick Cure in the Era of Feeling
R. D. Rosen
New York: Atheneum, 1977

Makes "fun" of people who believe in the immediate availability of well-being simply by communicating in a "feeling" way: For example,
I've really been getting in touch with myself lately.
I've struck some really deep chords.
I wish I could get into your head.

A New Guide to Rational Living
Albert Ellis and Robert A. Harper
N. Hollywood: Wilshire Book Co. (1977 edition)

Still, in my judgment, the most sensible and usable of the self-help books.

Public Works—A Handbook for Self Reliant Living
Edited and compiled by Valter Szykitka
: Links Books, 1974

A huge, fascinating collection of first aid, child care, survival hints taken from government sources. Have seen it around in stores that sell cut-rate books.

Bittersweet—Surviving and Growing from Loneliness
Terri Schultz
New York: T. Y. Crowell, 1976

Mature, reflective, poignant, helpful, and beautifully written. Not everything can be sweet.

Exuberance—A Philosophy of Happiness
Paul Kurtz
Buffalo: Prometheus, 1977

A great humanist handbook!

Four surprise books, religious in tone, humanist in spirit

Beginnings Without End—Sam Keen
With Open Hands—Henri J. M. Nouwen
The Season's People—A Book of Spiritual Teachings
by Stephen Gaskin
Whatever Became of Sin?—Karl Menninger

*The Twenty-Ninth Day—Accommodating Human
Needs and Numbers to the Earth's Resources*
    Lester R. Brown
    New York: W. W. Norton, 1978

    A very sensitive and important sober book on the
    pressures of limited earth resources by the leader of
    the Worldwatch Institute.

*Help—A Guide to Counseling and Therapy Without a
Hassle*
    Jane Marks
    New York: Julian Messner, 1976

    Just what it says. The focus is on young adults.

The Teenage Body Book
    Kathy McCoy and Charles Wibbelsman
    New York: Pocket Books, 1979.

    The best introduction to health and sex and good
    living for high school age youth.

College on Your Own
    Carl T. Parker and Gene R. Havers
    New York: Bantam Books, 1978

    Everything you need to know to apply independent
    studies toward college credit.

    Pursue a subject you've always wanted to know
    about.

You Are Not Alone
  Martin Grossack
  New York: Signet, 1978

  From the cover: The acclaimed guide to mental
  health, emotional balance, and sexual vitality using
  the teachings of Dr. Albert Ellis and the Institute for
  Rational Living.

  I agree that it's a really good, no-nonsense, self-help
  book.

Questions and Answers About Arabs and Jews
  Ira Hirschman
  New York: Bantam Books, 1977

  Reminds us of what actually happened in the last
  few years. Presents a point of view I agree with.

My favorite of all the books I've written is

YOU
  New York: Times Books, 1978.

  The Psychology of Surviving and Enhancing Your
        Social Life
        Love Life
        Sex Life
        School Life
        Work Life
        Home Life
        Emotional Life
        Creative Life
        Spiritual Life
        Style of Life
        Life

The next one of mine I like is

Psychology For You
  New York: Sadlier/Oxford, 1978

  A humanistic text with a lot of good stuff in it.

When someone asks you a question
and the answer is obvious
you could say,

Is the Pope Catholic?
Does gravity pull?
Does the sun shine?
Is the ocean deep?
Does F.A.O. Schwarz have toys?
Is Rockefeller rich?
Does a bear shit in the woods?

Any of the above is preferable
to saying, "Now that's a stupid
question."

PLACES TO GET FREE
OR INEXPENSIVE STUFF

Free catalogue of more than 250 government booklets
(mostly free) such as
  Backpacking in the National Forests
  Nutrition . . . Food at Work for You
  Save Energy—Save Money
  Removing Stains

  Send your name and address to
    Consumer Information Center
    Pueblo, Colorado 81009

The best catalogues for inexpensive books, prints, and
records (mainly publishers closeouts). Ask to be put on
mailing list.

  Publishers Central Bureau   Barnes and Noble
  1 Champion Avenue   105 Fifth Avenue
  Avenel, N.J. 07131   New York, N.Y. 10003

Get your name on the mailing list of the
  Superintendent of Documents
  U.S. Government Printing Office
  Washington, D.C. 20402

If you want to check up on charities you are not sure
about, write
  National Information Bureau
  419 Park Avenue South
  New York, N.Y. 10016

  or your local Better Business Bureau

If you want to take high school or college courses by
correspondence, write for "Study At Home." It lists
2,000 courses. Copies are $1.00 from
  National University Extension Association
  One Dupont Circle, Suite 360
  Washington, D.C. 20036

Free U.S. pamphlets offer vacation tips and how to register complaints.

Consumer Information
U.S. Travel Service
U.S. Dept. of Commerce
Washington, D.C. 20230

A guide to sources of financial help for college students is available for $.50.

American Legion National Emblem Sales
P.O. Box 1055
Indianapolis, Ind. 46206

Ask for "Need A Lift?"

For college students already enrolled—families can apply for a Basic Educational Opportunity Grant.

BEOG
P.O. Box B
Iowa City, Iowa 52230

A great list of records and cassettes, poets reading their own poems, recordings of condensed books, theatrical productions of Shakespeare.

Caedmon Records
505 Eighth Avenue
New York, N.Y. 10018

Center for Cassette Studies, 8110 Webb Ave., North Hollywood, Cal. 91605 has a 600-page catalogue of lectures and interviews on a wide range of topics including psychology, religion, and literature.

For a list of publications on energy policy, nuclear power, and alternative energy sources, write

Public Interest Research Group
P.O. Box 19312
Washington, D.C. 20036

For a complete publications list by the Public Citizen Health Research Group, write

Public Citizen
P.O. Box 19404
Washington, D.C. 20036

For a sample copy of *Critical Mass Journal,* the newspaper of the citizen's movement for safe and efficient energy, write
    Critical Mass Journal
    P.O. Box 1538
    Dept. P.C.
    Washington, D.C. 20013

For a sample copy of *Elements,* reporting on who owns and controls the world's natural resources, write
    James Ridgeway
    1747 Connecticut Ave., N.W.
    Washington, D.C. 20009

For a copy of the publication "Food is More Than Just Something to Eat" and for information on starting a food cooperative, write
    Department of Agriculture
    Office of Information
    14th St. and Independence Ave., S.W.
    Washington, D.C. 20250

For the publication "HEW and Civil Rights," write
    Office for Civil Rights
    Department of Health, Education and Welfare
    330 Independence Avenue, S.W.
    Washington, D.C. 20201

For publications dealing with the concerns of economically or politically oppressed persons in areas of education, housing, unemployment, civil rights, write
    Operation P.U.S.H.
    930 East 50th Street
    Chicago, Illinois 60615

For information on all aspects of women's rights, write
    Institute for Studies in Equality
    926 J Street
    Sacramento, Cal. 95814

For publications on air pollution, write
   Environmental Protection Agency
   Office of Public Affairs
   Waterside Mall
   401 M Street, S.W.
   Washington, D.C. 20460

The Gray Panthers at 3700 Chestnut St., Philadelphia, Pa. 19104, will send information on their programs concerned with aging and other issues affecting the elderly.

The Center for Science in the Public Interest will send sample copies of its newsletters, *CSPI Quarterly,* and *The Nutrition Newsletter,* as well as a publications list.
   CSPI
   1757 S St., N.W.
   Washington, D.C. 20009

For a pamphlet on the Freedom of Information Act and how to use it, write
   Freedom of Information Clearinghouse
   P.O. Box 19367
   Washington, D.C. 20036

The Alliance for Neighborhood Government bulletin contains information on neighborhood rights and responsibilities, issues, programs, models, and legislation. Send a first class stamp to
   ANG
   1901 O St., N.W.
   Washington, D.C. 20009

Useful toll-free hotlines

VD Hotline	800-523-1885 (U.S.)
	800-462-4996
	(Pennsylvania)
ACTION (volunteering for America)	800-621-4000 (except Washington, D.C.)
Runaway children can get counseling by calling	800-621-4000
If you suspect your car has a safety defect, call U.S. Dept. of Transportation.	800-424-9393 (except Hawaii and Alaska)
For complaints on discrimination in housing	800-424-8590 (U.S.)
	755-5490
	(Washington, D.C.)
Consumer Product Safety Commission (CPSC) Receives reports on injuries/ deaths related to hazardous manufactured products and assists consumers in evaluating safety of products on sale.	800-638-2666 (U.S.)
	800-492-2937
	(Maryland)
OSHA (Occupational Safety and Health Administration) Provides information to workers about OSHA and accepts reports about work-related accidents or dangerous working conditions.	800-555-1212 (ask for regional office number)
National Runaway Hotline. Advisory services to runaways and parents.	800-972-6004
National Solar Heating and Cooling Information Center	800-523-2929 (U.S.)
	800-462-4983
	(Pennsylvania)

Educational Grants Hotline Operated by Dept. of H.E.W.'s Office of Education.	800-638-6700
Federal Community Education **Clearinghouse** Also funded by Dept. of H.E.W.'s Office of Education.	800-638-6698 (U.S.) 700-3000 (Washington, D.C.)
United States Travel Service Supplies all kinds of travel information, accepts complaints, and provides information on special needs while traveling.	800-243-2372 (U.S.) 800-822-7611 (Connecticut)

SECTION
EIGHTEEN
HEROES
AND PLACES

Do heroes come alive anymore?

EIGHTEEN PEOPLE ALIVE TODAY
(WITH HEROIC DIMENSIONS)
WHOM I ADMIRE THE MOST

Norman Cousins
Mary Calderone
Albert Ellis
Bill Baird
Ralph Nader
Norman Lear
George Anne Geyer
Elie Wiesel
Sakharov
Gloria Steinem
Woodward and Bernstein
Erich Fromm
Roger Baldwin
Henry Morgenthaler
William Douglas
Ann Landers
Phil Donahue

SOME HEROES
BEFORE MY TIME

Benjamin Franklin
Thomas Jefferson
Lincoln Steffens
Thomas Paine
Emma Goldman
Big Bill Hayward
Havelock Ellis
Dorothea Dix
Upton Sinclair
Eugene V. Debs
Herman Melville
Harriet Tubman
Charles Darwin
Clarence Darrow
Mary Cassatt
Henry David Thoreau
Jack London
Mother Jones

Who are your heroes?

EIGHTEEN PEOPLE I
REMEMBER WITH ADMIRATION

When you read about their lives it's hard not to be disappointed to some extent. One likes one's heroes without blemishes. I have in mind a couple who proved disappointing in retrospect (John F. Kennedy and Franklin Roosevelt).

My list
Mahatma Gandhi (1869–1948)
     The inspired leader of India's independence movement once suggested that there were seven worldly sins:

> wealth without work,
> pleasure without conscience,
> knowledge without character,
> commerce without morality,
> science without humanity,
> worship without sacrifice,
> politics without principle.

The rest and a word or two
that comes to mind about them

Martin Luther King (1929–1968)	Freedom
Margaret Sanger (1879–1966)	Crusader
Albert Einstein (1879–1955)	Humble
Eleanor Roosevelt (1884–1962)	A Grand lady
Franklin Roosevelt (1882–1945)	Hope
Martin Buber (1878–1965)	Man of God
David Ben-Gurion (1886–1973)	Prophet

Bertrand Russell (1872–1970)	Philosopher
Paul Robeson (1898–1976)	Singer
John F. Kennedy (1917–1963)	Inspirational
Resistance fighter (World War II)	Hero
Norman Thomas (1884–1968)	Socialist
Sigmund Freud (1856–1939)	Liberator
George Bernard Shaw (1856–1950)	Wit
Charles Chaplin (1889–1977)	Bittersweet
International Brigade volunteer (Spanish Civil War)	Betrayed
Margaret Mead (1902–1978)	Feisty

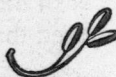

EIGHTEEN OF MY
FAVORITE MOVIES—SO FAR*

A Streetcar Named Desire

Citizen Kane

The Seven Beauties

The Gold Rush

Marty

The Grapes of Wrath

The Good Earth

King of Hearts

Rashomon

Children of Paradise

Outrageous

The Blue Angel

Annie Hall

Harold and Maude

The Bicycle Thief

City Lights

Potemkin

The Bakers' Wife

* As of October 1978. If you agree, check, and then add
others of your own preference.

EIGHTEEN IMPORTANT
NATIONAL ORGANIZATIONS
DEVOTED TO ENHANCEMENT OF
LIFE IN THIS COUNTRY

Write for catalogues or free publications—
Volunteer to help!

American Cancer Society, 777 Third Avenue, New York, N.Y. 10017

American Civil Liberties Union, 22 East 40th Street, New York, N.Y. 10016

American Red Cross, 17th and D Streets, N.W., Washington, D.C. 20006

Americans for Democratic Action, 1411 K Street, N.W., Washington, D.C. 20005

Anti-Defamation League of B'nai B'rith, 315 Lexington Avenue, New York, N.Y. 10016

Institute for Family Research and Education, 760 Ostrom Avenue, Syracuse, N.Y. 13210*

March of Dimes, 1275 Mamaroneck Avenue, White Plains, N.Y. 10605

Mental Health Association, 1800 North Kent Street, Arlington, Va. 22209

NAACP, 1790 Broadway, New York, N.Y. 10019

NARAL—National Abortion Rights Action League, 825 15th Street, N.W., Washington, D.C. 20005

National Council on Alcoholism, 733 Third Avenue, New York, N.Y. 10017

National Organization for Women, 425 13th Street, Suite 101, Washington, D.C. 20004

* This is where the author hangs out.

National Alliance for Optional Parenthood, 3 North Liberty Street, Baltimore, Md. 21201 (Write for their excellent pamphlet, "Am I Parent Material?")

Population Institute, 110 Maryland Avenue, N.E., Washington, D.C. 20002

Public Citizen (Ralph Nader), P.O. Box 19404, Washington, D.C. 20031*

Sex Information and Education Council of U.S. (SIECUS), 84 Fifth Avenue, Suite 407, New York, N.Y. 10011

World Future Society, 4916 St. Elmo Avenue (Bethesda), Washington, D.C. 20014

Zero Population Growth, 1346 Connecticut Avenue, N.W., Washington, D.C. 20036

---

* I'm very partial to this group. I urge you to join it!

EIGHTEEN BOOKS
RECENTLY BANNED IN SOME AMERICAN SCHOOLS AND LIBRARIES.
ALL ARE RECOMMENDED

John Steinbeck: Of Mice and Men

J. D. Salinger: Catcher in the Rye

Piri Thomas: Down These Mean Streets

Ernest Hemingway: For Whom the Bell Tolls
To Have and Have Not
A Farewell to Arms

Ken Kesey: One Flew Over the Cuckoo's Nest

Herman Hesse: Siddhartha

Kurt Vonnegut: Slaughterhouse Five

Alexander Solzhenitzyn: One Day in the Life of Ivan Denisovich

Bernard Malamud: The Fixer

Lewis Carroll: Alice in Wonderland

Mark Twain: Huckleberry Finn

Germaine Greer: The Female Eunuch

Malcolm X: The Autobiography of Malcolm X

Anthony Burgess: A Clockwork Orange

Ralph Ellison: The Invisible Man

Norman Mailer: Armies of the Night

EIGHTEEN NOVELS I'VE READ
WITH ENORMOUS EXCITEMENT

The eighteen (listed not exactly in order of "impact" but more or less) are:

Romain Rolland: Jean Christophe
Fyodor Dostoyevsky: The Brothers Karamazov
Thomas Mann: Buddenbrooks
Sholem Asch: Three Cities
Herman Melville: Billy Budd
John Dos Passos: U.S.A.
Albert Camus: The Stranger
Franz Kafka: Amerika
Gertrude Stein: Three Lives
André Malraux: Man's Fate
Virginia Woolf: Orlando
Somerset Maugham: The Razor's Edge
Evelyn Waugh: Brideshead Revisited
Saul Bellow: Herzog
Herman Melville: Moby Dick
Iris Murdoch: An Unofficial Rose
Thomas Hardy: The Mayor of Casterbridge
Erica Jong: Fear of Flying

EIGHTEEN IDIOTIC NOTIONS

You can be anything you want to be.

Everything occurs in cycles. We are just in a phase that has been experienced already.

People are meant for each other.

There is no such thing as luck.

Everything happens just as it is supposed to.

People know what they want out of life.

Love is blind.

The fact that there are differences between men and women entitles men to special privileges.

If you do the right thing you can be sure of just rewards.

The world owes you a living.

If you have not observed or understood it, it doesn't exist.

The "good old days" were better.

You can predict the future.

People can read minds.

Marriages are made in heaven.

There is only one religion that "saves."

Gun control is anti-American.

Everything happens to me.

EIGHTEEN PEOPLE AND IDEAS
I'M NOT IMPRESSED WITH,
BUT ALMOST EVERYBODY ELSE IS
*(that may mean there is
something wrong with me)*

Tolkien

Castaneda

The new narcissism

Carl Sagan

Social biology

Encounters of the
   third kind

B. F. Skinner

The Gothic novel

The top-rated TV
   shows ("Mork
   and Mindy" and
   "60 Minutes"
   excepted)

Astrology

The good old days

Being reborn

Every one of the new
   cults

Running

Punk rock

Biorhythm

Transcendental
   meditation

est

EIGHTEEN PEOPLE AND IDEAS I'M IMPRESSED WITH, BUT NOT EVERYBODY ELSE IS
(that may mean there is something wrong with them)

Public Citizen

SIECUS

The Bald Soprano

I and Thou

Moment

Garp

Small Is Beautiful

Rational-Emotive Therapy

The Search for the Full Human Being

ACLU

Bella Abzug

Kenneth C. Edelin

Choice (as against compulsory pregnancy)

The New York Times

Common Cause

Planned Parenthood

The Good Fence (Israel)

God

THE EIGHTEEN MOST MAGNIFICENT* HUMAN-MADE SIGHTS (NOT RUINS OR MUSEUMS) STILL TO BE SEEN IN THE WORLD TODAY.

Hurry, see them before pollution, wars, and modernization destroy them all.

Old city of Jerusalem
Bruges (Belgium)
New York City skyline
The Kremlin
King's Chapel (Cambridge, England)
The Grand Palace and temples of Bangkok
Kyoto (temples of)
The Sistine Chapel (Rome)
Notre Dame (France)
Statue of David (Florence)
St. Mark's Plaza (Venice)
San Francisco
The heart of Rome
The spirit of the Durham Cathedral (England)
The harbor of Sydney (with the Opera House)
The university in Mexico City
Old Amsterdam
So many memories crowd my mind that
    I can't decide on the last one.

* Restricted only by my own limited experience. You produce your own list.

YOUR
PERSONAL
SECTION

---

*The process of not learning
is exhausting.*

Respond with ink if you are pretty sure of your answers.

Respond with invisible ink if you don't want anyone else to see your answers.

Respond with pencil if you want to be free to change your mind before you are ready to purchase another copy of this book.

• •

Name three things that you would like to happen to you within the next few years.

1.

2.

3.

Mention something you'd like to happen to three people you know (even your parents).

1. _____

2. _____

3. _____

Mention three aspects of your personality that you think are fine.

1.

2.

3.

Name three characteristics that you have that
you'd like to improve.

1.

2.

3.

Select one of the above and decide how you are
going to do it (space for notes on how).

Mention one good deed you plan to do today.
(Thing of something. It could even be something
like saying "thank you" for breakfast to someone
who fixed it for you.)

Could you think of one step you could take today
to help you realize one of your future ambitions?
One Step:

What are some good things you know how to do?

1.

2.

3.

What are some things you wish you could do?

1.

2.

3.

Discover a way you can go about doing one of the things you don't know how to do.

END
SECTION

The end piece, "Where do we go from here?", is a collection of bits and pieces I've published elsewhere. Some of it was in *YOU* and some in *Psychology For You*. Before that, it was used in some of my talks. Some of it is new. The idea is that not everything has to be new.

My "new you" is made up of the old me with revised interpretations combined with new experiences that enhance my life.

WHERE DO WE GO FROM HERE?*

Sometimes I think the world is full of weirdos who claim to have solutions for everyone else's problems. With all the people offering us happiness through certain books, certain foods, certain prophets, or certain stars, it is little wonder that life is full of uncertainties.

Often I wonder whether human beings aren't so mixed up that they must put a lot of energy into getting themselves together. The less together they are, the more of their time is spent being unproductive and angry. Whether they know it or not, they are too angry for love or new experiences.

People who hate themselves hate a lot of people in the process. It took me a long time to discover this.

I remember one day of terrific insight, sitting

* This is my text for a multimedia tape and film strip developed with lyrics and music by Laurie and Peter Gollobin. Entitled "Getting It Together Is Life Itself," it is published by Educational Activities, Inc., P.O. Box 392, Freeport, N.Y. 11520.

around a pool with a friend. We wasted four hours talking about all the people we hated, until it dawned on us: All the people we hated were having a good time while we were talking about them. What a waste of time.

People who are messed up spend most of their time hurting themselves or others. They tend to do things that are against their best interests, repeating this behavior over and over again because, in a way, they can't help it.

Here are a few examples.

I know someone who spends most of her time thinking about the people who don't like her. The people who are supposed to dislike her don't even know she exists.

Another person finds his life irrelevant, the world meaningless. He spends most of his time sleeping, not doing his work, and quarreling with his brother and mother. He is so busy *not* doing things that he has no time for friends or pleasure.

Do you find yourself looking for yourself? What does that mean?

A lot of people come to me and say they can't find themselves, or that, for them, life has no meaning. They come to me and confess, "I've never been so lonely and unhappy in all my life."

238

What I say is . . . Life is not a meaning. It's an opportunity. Life is made up of a series of meaningful experiences, each of which often lasts for only a short time.

If you are in a situation that is bad, try to improve or change it. Some changes can be made quickly and easily. Others may take a long time. In that case, discover strategies of toleration or compromise. But whatever you do, don't punish yourself because of someone else's problems, or something that's out of your control. Pass that course you hate. Why suffer by having to take it over again? Don't continue a relationship only because you don't want to hurt the other person's feelings. This is punishing yourself *and* the other person, while you get a false sense of being nice.

It's easy to blame everything on an evil world, irrelevant school work, "having nothing to do." It's *easy* to feel rotten about yourself. But, really, no one can make you feel inferior without your consent. Sometimes you can't do much about the outside world, but sometimes you can. Waiting till tomorrow, and then I'll get it done, usually means that you won't. What you do now determines very largely what will happen to you in the future.

It's not so difficult to know when you're doing the wrong thing. Chances are that if you are not doing what is right for you, you will develop symptoms like . . . overdependency, overeating, overtalking, oversleeping, fear of high, low, tight, empty places, anxiety, underachieving, sexual hang-ups, loneliness, proneness to accidents, tension headaches. To say nothing about boasting, not having anything to do, or not ever enjoying being alone. And haven't you noticed that the process of not learning is exhausting? That doesn't mean you never feel nervous or depressed. It's hard work to make your life psychologically healthy.

The shift from a state of conflict to a state of health rarely occurs automatically or easily. Alcohol or other drugs don't do the job. If you drink or use drugs when you're feeling low, you'll feel high for a while. But when you come down later, nothing will have changed.

But life isn't all pain. If you see life as an opportunity, then it can be open to wondrous experiences. Whatever you decide to do with your life, it can be based on a wide range of alternatives. People who are striving to find meaning in a mature way are people whose lives are made up of meaningful choices. They often have more to do than they have time to do it in. They have alternatives. They take risks. They can enjoy being alone at times. And when they are in love, they know that it is often more important to meet the needs of another person than to satisfy their own impulses.

Don't decide in advance about all the things you hate and will always hate. New experiences help you make choices. In fact, a good time to try a new experience is when you're feeling depressed.

Look at all the things you could do right now:

Keep a diary. Remember dreams. Learn a new word. Photograph trees. Write a poem. Write two poems. Fly a kite. Run a mile. Decide on a country to visit in Europe, read all about it, and then figure out how you're going to get there. Read a book like *The Thorn Birds* and ask yourself why so many people liked such a strange novel. Write me a letter. Write a letter to someone you owe a letter to. Go mountain climbing. See a foreign film—a Chaplin film. Explore why some people think Andy Warhol is a genius and some people think he's cracked. Say hello to a person you think you should hate.

People who are bored are boring.

People who are down on themselves are boring to be with.

Live a little.

Life is not a meaning. It's an opportunity.

Getting it together is life itself.

BEGINNING AGAIN

If you get hung up
anywhere

Hang up
and try me again later.

Parting shot to a young friend:
"Just because you are
unhappy is no excuse to
make yourself unhappier"

ABOUT THE AUTHOR

DR. SOL GORDON teaches child and family studies, and is the director of the prominent Institute for Family Research and Education in Syracuse. He is the author of *You: A Survival Guide for Youth, The Sexual Adolescent, Parenting: A Guide for Young People* and *You Would If You Loved Me.* His books, television appearances and lectures have earned him the trust and respect of teenagers, parents, grandparents and fellow educators everywhere.

MS READ-a-thon–
a simple way
to start youngsters reading.

Boys and girls between 6 and 14 can join the MS READ-a-thon and help find a cure for Multiple Sclerosis by reading books. And they get two rewards — the enjoyment of reading, and the great feeling that comes from helping others.

Parents and educators: For complete information call your local MS chapter, or call toll-free (800) 243-6000. Or mail the coupon below.

Kids can help, too!

Mail to:
National Multiple Sclerosis Society
205 East 42nd Street
New York, N.Y. 10017
I would like more information about the MS READ-a-thon and how it can work in my area.

MS
Mystery
Sleuth

Name_____
(please print)
Address_____
City_____State_____Zip_____
Organization_____

BA—10/77

Bantam
On Psychology

☐	12196	**PASSAGES: Predictable Crises of Adult Life,** Gail Sheehy	$2.75
☐	10492	**HOW TO SURVIVE THE LOSS OF A LOVE,** Colgrove, Bloomfield, et. al.	$1.95
☐	11865	**THE GESTALT APPROACH & EYE WITNESS TO THERAPY,** Fritz Perls	$2.25
☐	11656	**KICKING THE FEAR HABIT,** Manuel J. Smith	$2.25
☐	12878	**THE BOOK OF HOPE,** DeRosis & Pellegrino	$2.50
☐	12109	**THE PSYCHOLOGY OF SELF-ESTEEM: A New Concept of Man's Psychological Nature,** Nathaniel Branden	$2.25
☐	12331	**WHAT DO YOU SAY AFTER YOU SAY HELLO?** Eric Berne, M.D.	$2.50
☐	10470	**GESTALT THERAPY VERBATIM,** Fritz Perls	$2.25
☐	12367	**PSYCHO-CYBERNETICS AND SELF-FULFILLMENT,** Maxwell Maltz, M.D.	$2.25
☐	10537	**THE FIFTY-MINUTE HOUR,** Robert Lindner	$1.95
☐	10562	**AWARENESS: Exploring, Experimenting, Experiencing,** John O. Stevens	$2.25
☐	12217	**THE DISOWNED SELF,** Nathaniel Branden	$2.25
☐	11756	**CUTTING LOOSE: An Adult Guide for Coming to Terms With Your Parents,** Howard Halpern	$2.25
☐	12725	**BEYOND FREEDOM AND DIGNITY,** B. F. Skinner	$2.75
☐	12553	**WHEN I SAY NO, I FEEL GUILTY,** Manuel Smith	$2.50
☐	11519	**IN AND OUT OF THE GARBAGE PAIL** Fritz Perls	$2.25

Buy them at your local bookstore or use this handy coupon for ordering:

Bantam Books, Inc., Dept. ME, 414 East Golf Road, Des Plaines, Ill. 60016

Please send me the books I have checked above. I am enclosing $_____
(please add 75¢ to cover postage and handling). Send check or money order
—no cash or C.O.D.'s please.

Mr/Mrs/Miss_____

Address_____

City_____State/Zip_____

ME—3/79
Please allow four weeks for delivery. This offer expires 9/79.

Bantam Book Catalog

Here's your up-to-the-minute listing of over 1,400 titles by your favorite authors.

This illustrated, large format catalog gives a description of each title. For your convenience, it is divided into categories in fiction and non-fiction——gothics, science fiction, westerns, mysteries, cookbooks, mysticism and occult, biographies, history, family living, health, psychology, art.

So don't delay——take advantage of this special opportunity to increase your reading pleasure.

Just send us your name and address and 50¢ (to help defray postage and handling costs).

BANTAM BOOKS, INC.
Dept. FC, 414 East Golf Road, Des Plaines, Ill. 60016

Mr./Mrs./Miss_____
(please print)

Address_____

City_____State_____Zip_____

Do you know someone who enjoys books? Just give us their names and addresses and we'll send them a catalog too!

_____

Mr./Mrs./Miss_____

Address_____

City_____State_____Zip_____

_____

Mr./Mrs./Miss_____

Address_____

City_____State_____Zip_____

FC—9/78